new edition

English network

Basic Conversation

Michele Charlton und Carolyn Kilday Wittmann

Langenscheidt

Berlin · München · Wien · Zürich
London · Madrid · New York · Warschau

English Network Basic Conversation

Autorinnen:
Michele Charlton
Carolyn Kilday Wittmann

Beratende Mitwirkung:
Jutta Sendzik, Wernigerode

Verlagsredaktion:
Claudia Schwarz

Grafik und Layout:
Iris Steiner, Design Im Kontor, München
Umschlag: Sabine Nasko, München
kaltner verlagsmedien GmbH, Bobingen

Lehrwerkskomponenten:

Kursbuch	50 468
Audio-CD	57 766
Lehrerhandreichungen	50 469
Activity Book	50 508
Pocket Grammar A2	50 509
Pocket Grammar B1	50 514
Pocket Reader	50 505
Pocket Get in touch	50 664
Pocket Short Stories A2	50 662
Pocket Traveller	50 666
Pocket Vocabulary	50 663

www.langenscheidt.de/englishnetwork

Druck und Bindung: Stürtz GmbH, Würzburg

ISBN 978-3-526-50468-9

11061

Welcome
to *English Network Basic Conversation*

Sie haben schon eine ganze Menge Grundkenntnisse im Englischen und möchten diese nun in Gesprächen im persönlichen Kontext anwenden? Dann liegen Sie mit *English Network Basic Conversation* genau richtig! Mit diesem Kurs trainieren Sie besonders die mündlichen Fertigkeiten Sprechen und Hören und setzen Ihr Wissen in Alltagsgesprächen praktisch ein.

Was ist das Besondere an *Basic Conversation*?

Mit diesem Kursbuch lernen Sie, sich aktiv an Gesprächen zu beteiligen, Ihre Meinung auszudrücken, Kommentare zu geben, ein Gespräch am Laufen zu halten und Vieles mehr. Im Mittelpunkt jeder Unit steht ein Thema aus dem Alltag, das aus einem neuen, ungewöhnlichen Blickwinkel heraus betrachtet wird. Dabei geht es ebenso um den Tagesablauf, eine mehr oder weniger gesunde Lebensweise wie um die Urlaubsplanung oder die täglichen Tücken der Technik. Sie trainieren also, Gespräche in Ihrem persönlichen Lebensumfeld zu führen.

Wie ist *Basic Conversation* aufgebaut?

English Network Basic Conversation ist in 12 Units und eine Einführung *(Getting Started)* gegliedert. Jede Unit besteht aus 3 Seiten, die Sie im Kurs behandeln und aus einer Seite *Selfstudy* für die Nachbereitung zu Hause. Das Schwergewicht liegt in allen Teilen auf den mündlichen Fertigkeiten. Immer, wenn Sie folgendes Symbol sehen, haben Sie die Möglichkeit, selber etwas auf Englisch zu sagen. In jeder Unit wird ein Aspekt, der im Gespräch eine wichtige Rolle spielt, besonders betont. Diese Übungen sind jeweils mit **What to say** gekennzeichnet. Im *Selfstudy* bekommen Sie Tipps, wie man sich in Gesprächen mit englischsprachigen Menschen richtig verhält.

In den beiden *Extras* bekommen Sie interessante Hintergrundinformationen zu Wales und den Provinzen Ostkanadas. Bei einem Quiz können Sie jeweils Ihre Vorkenntnisse einbringen, die anschließend um vielfältige Fakten bereichert werden.

Zusätzlich können Sie Ihr Vokabular zu jedem Themenbereich systematisch festigen und erweitern, in dem Sie in jeder Unit mit dem *Topic Vocabulary* im Anhang arbeiten. Hier werden auch nützliche interkulturelle Besonderheiten thematisiert.

Und falls Sie doch mal etwas Unterstützung im Bereich Grammatik brauchen, haben wir für Sie einen *Grammar Check* entworfen, in dem Sie Regeln nachsehen und direkt selbst anwenden können.

Welches Begleitmaterial gibt es?

Begleitend zum Kursbuch gibt es eine Audio-CD, auf der Sie die Texte aus den Units wie auch die *Pronunciation*-Übungen und *Listenings* aus dem *Selfstudy*-Teil finden.

Wir wünschen Ihnen nun viel Freude beim Englischlernen und interessante Gespräche

Michele Charlton
Carolyn Kilday Wittmann

Michele Charlton
Carolyn Kilday Wittmann
und Ihr Verlag
Langenscheidt English Language Teaching

Contents

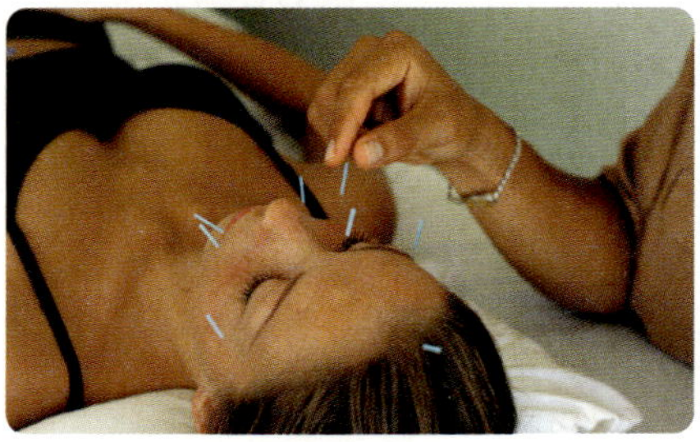

Contents

Symbols:

12 — The text and activity / exercise is on the CD. The number refers to the track number on the CD.

Speaking activity

p. 80 — There is a key, and the page number is given.

→ L & C — Language and culture

Getting started

1 Names

Ask questions to find out about other people's names: *Do you shorten your name?* If someone answers *yes*, then write his / her name on the line and ask for some more information.

Why did you shorten it?

What do most people call you?

Write a different name on each line, if possible.

Name		Extra Information
....	shortens his / her first name.	....
....	has or had a nickname.	....
....	is called after someone in his / her family.	....
....	has got an unusual first name or family name.	....
....	has got one or more middle names.	....
....	has got a name he / she dislikes.	....
....	changed his / her name when he / she got married.	....

Getting started

2 What to say: Introducing someone else

Look at the following phrases. Which one would you use in a more formal situation?

This is ... .
Have you met ...?
Do you know ...?
Can I introduce you to ...?

Look at the replies. Number them 1-4 from the most informal to the most formal.

- ☐ Hello.
- ☐ Hi.
- ☐ Pleased to meet you.
- ☐ Nice to meet you.

Now introduce someone to the class and say something about his / her name.

A: *Have you met Anna-Regina?*
B: *Hello.*
A: *She shortens her name. It's a bit long so most people call her Anni.*

3 Getting to know each other

First write down three or four words or phrases that say something about you.

taxi driver,
mother,
I love cats,
volleyball fan

In small groups show each other your words.
Ask questions to find out more about each other's words and phrases.
Now tell the class a few things about someone in your group.

4 What are you interested in?

- listening to music
- eating out
- sport
- pets
- films
- DIY
- computers
- reading
- cooking
- cars

Underline some of the things you are interested in. Find someone else in the class who has underlined some of the things that you are interested in. Sit down together, ask each other questions and find out more about what you have in common.

5a Why are you doing a conversation course?

Talk to people in the class and find out why they have decided to do a conversation course. How many different reasons did you hear? Tell the class.

5b Speaking a foreign language

Klaus, Fiona and Emma are doing a summer language course. Klaus is learning English and Emma and Fiona are doing a German course.

2 Listen to their conversation about speaking in a foreign language. What problems do they have?

Do you have similar problems or do you have different ones? Talk in small groups.

2 Listen again. Fiona and Klaus mention two ways which help to improve their English. What are they?

Do you think they are good ideas? What other ways can you think of to help you to improve your speaking, vocabulary, pronunciation, etc.?

6 What to say: Useful classroom phrases

If you are having problems speaking and understanding, here are some phrases you can use. Match a phrase on the left with a phrase with a similar meaning on the right.

1 Sorry, that was a bit too fast.	☐	I didn't quite understand what you said.
2 Sorry, I couldn't quite follow that.	☐	Can you spell that for me, please?
3 Can you repeat that, please?	☐	What's ... in English?
4 How do you say ... in English?	☐	Could you say that again, please?
5 What does ... mean?	☐	Can you speak more slowly, please?
6 Sorry, how do you spell that?	☐	I'm afraid, I don't understand the word ... .

Which ones are new for you?

7 A last question

Is there something you'd like to ask your teacher or someone in the class before you leave? Write down one or two questions and then ask and answer in class.

Peter, how did you get your nickname?

Susan, how many other English courses do you teach?

8 Bye bye

Just before you leave, say goodbye.

- *Bye, bye.*
- *Nice to have met you.*
- *See you next week / next lesson.*
- *It was nice to see you again.*

1 Everyday life

1 Everyday habits

http://www.factsfactsfacts.com/

Home
> music
> food
> **habits**
> sport
> people
> animals

> According to a survey of television viewing habits, Germans spend an average of 5 hours 33 minutes per week watching television. That's about an hour longer per week than in 1991.

> In an American online opinion poll 31% of people interviewed didn't need an alarm clock to get out of bed, but 27% had to press the snooze button three times before they were able to get up.

> American adults consume on average about 1.7 cups of coffee per day whereas Germans drink almost 3 cups per day. The Finns drink the most – more than 4 cups per day.

Look at the following sentences and tick (✔) the correct box.

	True	False
• I drink too much coffee.	☐	☐
• I often lose things.	☐	☐
• I frequently write lists.	☐	☐
• I'm usually on time.	☐	☐
• I rarely use the Internet.	☐	☐
• I find it difficult to get up in the mornings.	☐	☐
• I watch too much television.	☐	☐
• I usually tidy up as soon as I make a mess.	☐	☐
• I do most things at the last minute.	☐	☐
• I have about eight hours sleep per night.	☐	☐

In groups of three, take it in turns to read out those sentences that are true for you. The others should react, add information, etc.

Me too. I feel terrible in the mornings. I need a cup of coffee and …

Oh, I don't. I'm a morning person. I usually go for a jog …

Tell each other which habits you'd like to change.

2 Topic vocabulary: Everyday life

Did you find it easy to think of the right words? The *Topic vocabulary* will remind you of some useful words and phrases. Have a quick look and find the following:

- an activity you like doing
- an activity you don't like doing
- a word / phrase that describes how you feel at this moment
- how you say *ein Baby bekommen* in English
- a word or phrase you don't understand (and find out what it means)

→ **Topic vocabulary, p. 66**

3 Everyday sounds

3 Listen to the following sounds that you might hear in your daily life. What are they? Write a list. *dog barking ...*

Look at the sounds on your list and decide when you hear them. There are some useful time phrases in the *Topic vocabulary*.

Now talk to your partner. Tell each other when and where you hear these sounds and what part they play in your daily routine.

Encourage your partner to speak by asking questions.
e.g. *Does it annoy you?*
How often do you ...?
Do you enjoy ...?

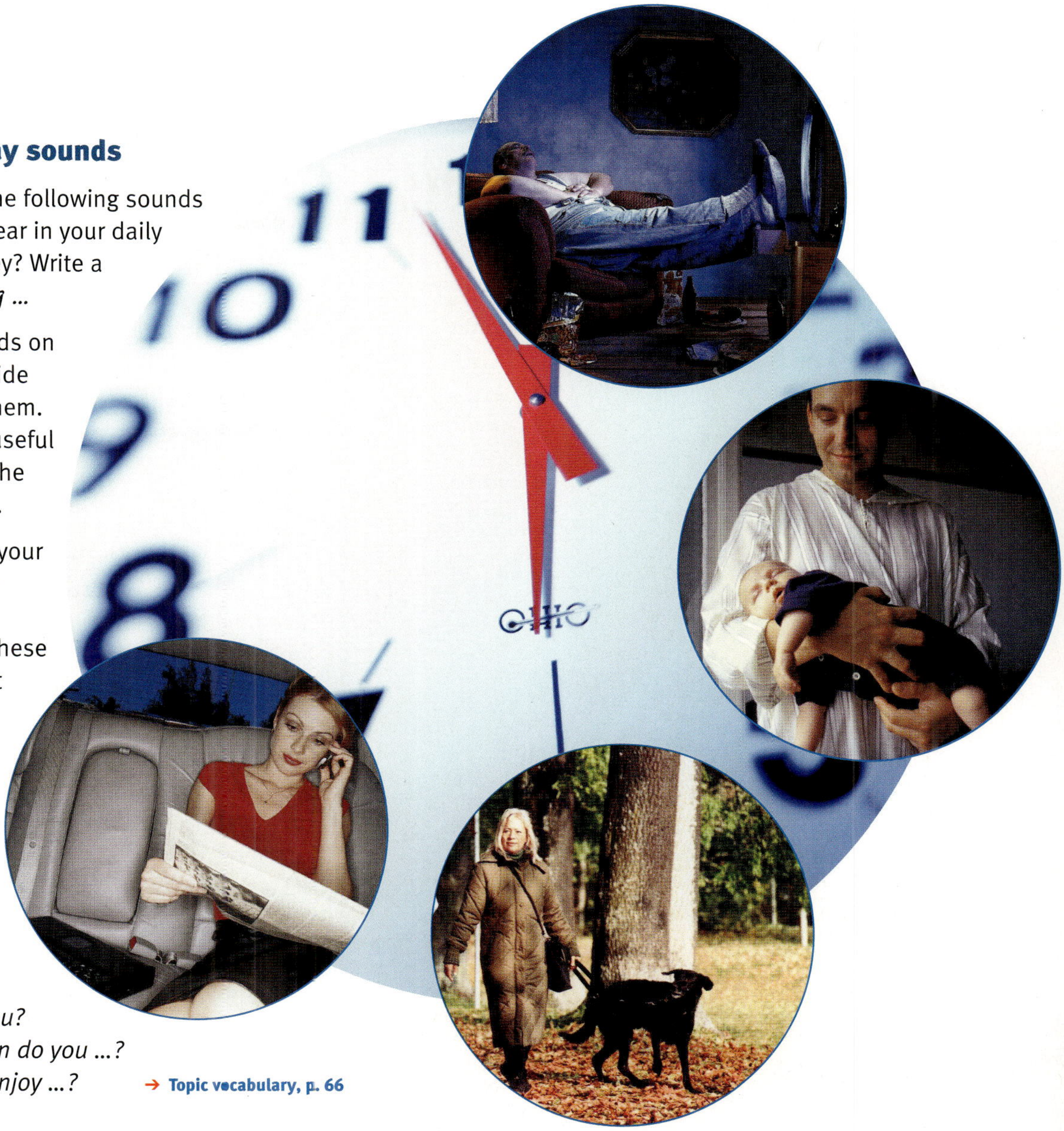

→ Topic vocabulary, p. 66

4a What to say: Starting a conversation

You meet someone you know. Here are three ways of starting the conversation.

Hello, how are you? ....

Hello, how are things? ....

Hi, I haven't seen you for ages. ....

How could you reply to each one? Write down your ideas.

4 Listen to the following people starting a conversation and talking about their everyday lives. Are their replies the same as yours?

4 Now listen again and write down one or two things each person says about his / her life at the moment. Is anything similar happening to you at the moment?

Here are some expressions people used:
Congratulations! *I'm sorry to hear that.* *Oh no!* *That's good news.* *Lucky you.*

How might you react to the following?
- I passed my driving test last week.
- My girlfriend is going into hospital next week.
- I'm flying to Madrid on Saturday.

→ L & C, p.66

4b What to say: Ending a conversation and saying goodbye

5 Listen to these people saying goodbye and fill in the missing words.

1 **A:** I .... I'm on the way to the hospital.
B: Say .... Joan for me.
A: Yes, will do.
B: And I .... soon. Bye.

2 **A:** Erm, I'm afraid .... now.
B: Yes, I'll let you .... work. See you later.
A: Bye.

3 **A:** Well, it's been .... to you again.
B: Yes, maybe we .... sometime.
A: Good idea. Give ....
B: OK. Bye.

Listen again and pay particular attention to the intonation. Practise the short exchanges in pairs.

5 Everyday conversation

Write down some things that are happening / have just happened / are going to happen in your life – at home, at work, to you, to your family or friends.

You are at a party and want to chat to a few of your friends about what is happening to you at the moment. Stand up and find a partner. Greet your partner, tell him / her what you're doing at the moment and react to what he/she is saying. When your teacher tells you to stop, say goodbye and find a new partner to talk to.

remember Use the **present progressive** to talk about something happening around now:
- *We're having problems with the computer.*

a future arrangement:
- *She's leaving next week.*

→ Grammar, p. 88

6 Out of the ordinary

What events upset our routine for a while or make a change to our daily lives? Brainstorm in class.

First ask your teacher, then talk in small groups. Find out
- what exceptional events have happened to them, their family or friends
- how it affected their daily routine
- if it has had any long-term effects on their everyday lives

6 Further ideas:
- new job
- overnight visitors
- new pet
- serious illness
- wedding
- divorce

Tip **Ending a conversation**

Before saying goodbye to someone, it is polite to signal that you are going to finish the conversation and leave, e.g. *Erm, I'm afraid I've got to go now*. A sudden *goodbye* without warning can sound impolite.

1 What to say: Saying goodbye

What do B and D say? Complete the two dialogues with the following sentences.

- Say hello to Frank for me.
- Yes, it's been really nice talking to you, too.
- Bye. See you next week.
- Yes, good idea. Give me a ring sometime.
- Yes, it's already six o'clock. I'll let you get back to your family.
- Bye. And don't forget to ring.

1 A: Oh, is that the time? I must rush.
B: ....
A: Yeah, they're waiting for their dinner.
B: ....
A: Yes, will do. Bye.
B: ....

2 C: Well, it was lovely to see you again.
D: ....
C: And we must get together one evening.
D: ....
C: Okay, I've got your phone number. Bye.
D: ....

2 Pronunciation: The sound [ə]

The [ə] is a very common sound in English. It is only used in *unstressed* syllables.

6 Listen to these words. The stressed syllables are underlined. Each circle marks an [ə] sound.

later German again together

First underline the stressed syllable in each word. Then put a circle around the /ə/ sounds.

1 sister 4 afraid 7 lesson
2 cassette 5 accent 8 tonight
3 even 6 pregnant 9 breakfast

7 Listen and check your pronunciation.

3 Vocabulary: *Do*, *get* and *have*

married	problems	a baby
the gardening	the housework	divorced
a language course	a chat	home

Complete these diagrams with the correct words from the box.

do
....
....
....

get
....
....
....

have
....
....
....

Now complete the sentences with one of the verb phrases in the correct tense.

1 I .... quite late because there was an accident on the motorway.
2 My English isn't very good so I'm going to ....
3 My sister has just .... It's a little boy.
4 I always .... on Saturdays. First I tidy up and then I hoover.
5 They're .... in May. I've just had an invitation to the wedding.
6 I really like talking to her. We often .... after work.

p. 78

2 People around us

1 How did you meet?

Write down the names of some of the following:

- your husband / wife / partner / girlfriend / boyfriend
- one of your oldest friends
- a close friend
- a work colleague
- a neighbour

Try to remember when, where and how you first met. Look at the *Topic vocabulary* for some time and place phrases.

Walk around and tell other students about the first time you met some of these people. React and show interest when other people are talking to you.

Really?
Yes.
Is that right?

Tell the class one piece of interesting information you heard.

→ Topic vocabulary, p. 67

2a People in our lives: A radio interview

You'll hear part of an American phone-in radio programme called "Important People in our Lives". The studio guest today is Maria, a British jazz singer.

8 Listen and make a list of the people Maria mentions who play a role in her life. Compare your lists in class.

8 Listen again and note down why the people on your list are important to her.

Look at the *Useful phrases* in the *Topic vocabulary*. Which of these phrases did Maria use?

→ Topic vocabulary, p. 67

2b I spend a lot of time with ...

What about you? Look at the questions below and tick (✔) the appropriate box(es).
Which of these people do you

	friend	neighbour	work colleague	relative	none of these
spend a lot of time with?	☐	☐	☐	☐	☐
rely on in an emergency?	☐	☐	☐	☐	☐
go on holiday with?	☐	☐	☐	☐	☐
do free time activities with?	☐	☐	☐	☐	☐
often write to or phone?	☐	☐	☐	☐	☐
invite to your house?	☐	☐	☐	☐	☐
lend your car to?	☐	☐	☐	☐	☐
borrow money from?	☐	☐	☐	☐	☐

Talk about your choices with one or two other students and give some details.

→ L & C, p. 67

3a What to say: Making yourself understood

Maria has got a new German neighbour, Christoph. Communication is sometimes a problem but they usually manage to make themselves understood.

9 Listen to the dialogue. What two communication problems do they have?

Look at the following useful phrases.

Correcting yourself	Showing you have understood
☐ Sorry, I'll start again.	☐ Oh, I see.
☐ What I mean is ...	☐ I've got it now.
☐ I'll try and say that again.	☐ That's quite clear now.

9 Listen again and tick the phrases you hear.

3b What about you?

Have you ever experienced a similar misunderstanding when speaking in a foreign language?

- in class
- at work
- on the phone
- on holiday

What happened? Tell the class.

4 Interesting people

Look at the following photos. Who would you like to read more about? Do they remind you of anyone you know?

More and more younger women want tattoos.

Former Superman helped raise millions for medical research and was active in Hollywood, starring and directing in TV projects until his death.

On April 14, 2002, Jenny Wood-Allen completed the London Marathon, aged 90 years 145 days.

You want to tell the others about someone you consider to be interesting or unusual, or someone you admire in some way. It could be:

- a person you know
- someone in your neighbourhood or area
- someone you've heard or read about

What words do you need? Write about ten words or phrases down. If you're not sure of the word in English, ask your teacher or another student or look in a dictionary or the *Topic vocabulary*.

→ **Topic vocabulary, p. 67**

In small groups, tell each other about your person. While listening, show interest and ask one or two questions. Use the phrases in activity 3a or in *Getting Started* (activity 6) if communication breaks down.

5 Could you imagine?

Could you imagine doing something out of the ordinary? In small groups, discuss how you would feel in the following situations. What problems might you encounter? Can you imagine any of your family or friends doing something similar?

1 You are in your mid-fifties and decide you need a new challenge in life. You want to open your own business.
2 Your mother-in-law comes to live with you.
3 You have two small children. You and your partner decide that the man should stay at home and look after the children while the woman goes out to work.
4 You marry someone who is twenty years older than you.

remember Be careful which tense you use in the **second conditional:**

- *If my mother-in-law* ***moved in, I'd move out.***
- *If I* ***stayed*** *at home, I* ***would have to*** *give up my career.*

→ **Grammar, p. 91**

1 What to say: Useful phrases

Complete these sentences and questions.

1 Two ways of saying you don't understand what someone says

a) Sorry, I couldn't q............... f............... that.

b) I'm a............... I d............... q............... understand w............... y............... said.

2 Two ways of asking someone to repeat

a) Could you s............... t............... a..............., please?

b) Sorry, c............... you r............... t..............., p...............?

3 Two ways of asking someone to speak more slowly

a) S..............., that was a b............... t............... f............... .

b) C............... you s............... more s..............., p...............?

4 Two ways of correcting what you have said

a) Sorry, I'll s............... a............... . b) W............... I m............... is ...

5 Two ways of saying that you have understood

a) Oh, I s............... . b) I've g............... it n............... .

> **Tip** **Finding the right tone**
> English speakers often use *I'm afraid* or *Sorry* to sound more friendly and polite. *I don't understand* or *You speak too quickly* would be too direct.
> A phrase like *I'm afraid I didn't quite follow that* shows that it is no one's fault that you didn't understand, and creates the right tone.

2 Pronunciation: Voiced sounds [dʒ], [v], [z], [ð] and voiceless sounds [tʃ], [f], [s], [θ]

Are the sounds in bold the same (✔) or different (✘)?

1 ☐ **j**ob / **G**erman	4 ☐ **th**is / **th**ing	7 ☐ nie**c**e / **s**ister	10 ☐ li**f**e / li**v**e
2 ☐ **ch**ess / **j**azz	5 ☐ **th**at / **th**ree	8 ☐ clo**s**ed / clo**s**e friend	
3 ☐ mana**g**er / emer**g**ency	6 ☐ **th**ick / **s**ick	9 ☐ o**ff** / o**f**	

10 Now listen to the words and check your pronunciation. Put a circle round the voiced sounds. When you make the voiced sound, you can feel your vocal cords vibrating.

3 Vocabulary: People – Who's who?

Complete the sentences with words that were in Unit 2.

1 Fiona is a close friend, not just an _ _ _ _ _ _ _ _ _ _ _ _ .

2 Her daughter's just had a little boy. It's her first _ _ _ _ _ _ _ _ _ .

3 She only has one niece and one _ _ _ _ _ _ . They're her sister's children.

4 She's just got divorced from her second _ _ _ _ _ _ _ . I wonder who'll be the third!

5 Marc's a _ _ _ _ _ _ _ _ _ of mine. We work in the same office.

6 His ex-wife says she'll never marry again, but she's got a new _ _ _ _ _ _ _ .

7 I have problems with my elder brother, but his wife is my favourite _ _ _ _ _ _-_ _-_ _ _ .

4 Please match

Find the expressions which mean more or less the same.

1 We don't see each other very often.	☐ a) We're great friends.
2 We became friends at university.	☐ b) We write or phone regularly.
3 I spend a lot of time with her.	☐ c) We seldom meet.
4 We keep in touch.	☐ d) We do quite a lot together.
5 We get on very well.	☐ e) We got to know each other when we were studying.

p. 78

3 Getting around

1 A transport survey

Transport Survey

You have been chosen to take part in our survey. We need basic information about what type of transport people use and for what purposes. Please help us by answering the questions. Thank you!

① How often do you use the following types of transport? Tick where appropriate

	more than once a week	a few times a month	a few times a year	rarely	never
car	○	○	○	○	○
taxi	○	○	○	○	○
bus / tram	○	○	○	○	○
underground	○	○	○	○	○
train	○	○	○	○	○
bicycle	○	○	○	○	○
plane	○	○	○	○	○
ferry	○	○	○	○	○
Other: Please state	○	○	○	○	○

② What type of transport do you usually use for

a) work ....

b) evening classes ....

c) shopping ....

d) social activities ....

e) holidays ....

③ How much time do you spend travelling on

a) an average weekday ....

b) an average weekend ....

Ask each other the questions on your survey. The first two sections of the *Topic vocabulary* will remind you of some useful phrases.

→ Topic vocabulary, p. 68

Were you surprised by any of the answers you heard? Tell the class.

→ L & C, p. 68

2a What to say: Agreeing and disagreeing

Tick the correct response to each statement.

Statement	Agreeing	Statement	Disagreeing
I'm afraid of flying.	☐ So am I. ☐ So have I. ☐ So do I.	I like taking the ferry.	☐ I'm not. ☐ But I haven't. ☐ Oh, I don't.
I wouldn't like to drive an automatic.	☐ Neither can I. ☐ Neither did I. ☐ Neither would I.	I can never find a parking space.	☐ Oh, I can. ☐ But I would. ☐ I did.

! Note: Use the same auxiliary (*am, can, have,* etc.) in the statement and in the answer. When there is no auxiliary, use *do* (for present simple) or *did* (for past simple).

2b What to say: Adding a comment

11 Listen and write down the man's responses to the statements.

	Man's response	Your response
I don't use public transport very much.		
I'd like to have a motorbike.		
I've never had a parking ticket.		

How would you respond? Write down a short response and a comment. Compare answers in class.

In pairs, have similar exchanges starting with the following statements. Agree or disagree and make a comment.

- I have / have never been in a helicopter.
- I'd / wouldn't like a trip in a hot-air balloon.
- I'm never / sometimes / often carsick.
- I enjoy / don't enjoy long journeys.
- I never / sometimes / often ride my bike in the city centre.
- I took my driving test when I was ...

3a Vocabulary: Travelling

Work in small groups. What words or phrases do you think of when you look at each of the three photos? You have two minutes to write down as many words as possible. Compare your lists in class.

Look at the *Topic vocabulary*. Can you find another word to go with each picture? → Topic vocabulary, p. 68

3b Likes and dislikes

Talk in groups of three about a type of transport

- you usually like using
- you often dislike using
- you used to like but don't like anymore
- would like to use more often

Try and use some of the phrases from activity 2a (*So do I*, etc.).

What did people dislike about travelling by train, by plane and by car? Tell the class about some of the things you heard.

remember Verbs of like and dislike are usually followed by the **gerund (–ing)**:

- *I enjoy cycling when the weather's nice.*
- *I can't stand driving in the rush hour.*

But use the **infinitive** after would like / love / hate / prefer:

- *I'd like to travel by train more often.*

→ Grammar, p. 93

4 A nightmare journey

In class, make a list of things that can turn a journey into a nightmare, e.g. the flight is delayed, your car breaks down.

12 Listen to Lynne talking to her friend Brian about a nightmare journey and note down three or four things that happened. Does she mention any of the things on your list?

12 Listen again. What questions and responses does Brian use to show interest and to encourage Lynne to keep talking?

Tell each other about a bad or unusual journey you've had. Use some of the questions and responses from the listening.

remember Use the **past progressive** to describe a scene:

- *It was raining.*

to talk about an activity in progress:

- *I was just falling asleep when the train stopped.*

The train stopped

I was falling asleep

→ Grammar, p. 89

Tip **Me too**

Although it is very common to use *So* and *Neither* when agreeing with someone, you will also hear native speakers using the more informal *Me too* or *Me neither*, e.g.

I love driving. *Me too.*
I didn't enjoy the trip. *Me neither.*

1 What to say: Agreeing and disagreeing

Continue the dialogues. First find a short response from box 1. Then add a comment from box 2.

1	2
So do I.	My husband's giving me a lift.
So did I.	Especially in good weather.
Oh, I'm not.	I don't like heights.
Oh, I haven't.	But I must buy one next week.
Neither can I.	Everyone drives too fast.
Neither would I.	It was very cheap.

1 A: I love cycling.
B: ....
2 A: I can't stand driving on the motorway.
B: ....
3 A: I've bought a season ticket for the underground.
B: ....
4 A: I booked my flight on the Internet.
B: ....
5 A: I'm taking the bus today.
B: ....
6 A: I wouldn't like to go in a hot-air balloon.
B: ....

2 Vocabulary: Which words go together?

1 signals	☐	a) test
2 traffic	☐	b) connection
3 public	☐	c) limit
4 rush	☐	d) jam
5 connecting	☐	e) collector
6 speed	☐	f) transport
7 driving	☐	g) hour
8 train	1	h) failure
9 ticket	☐	i) flight

3 Pronunciation: Stress

In words with two or more syllables, one syllable is pronounced more strongly than the rest. Underline the part of the word where the main stress falls like this: *transport*.

1 bicycle	5 travelling
2 appropriate	6 connection
3 automatic	7 roadworks
4 balloon	8 apparently

13 Listen to these words, then check your answers in the *Key*.

One word in a phrase also has greater stress. In B's responses underline the word which you think has greater stress. Do it like this:
A: *He isn't going home.* B: *But she is.*

A: I'm sometimes airsick.	B: So am I.
A: She isn't afraid of flying.	B: Neither is he.
A: They wouldn't do it.	B: But we would.
A: I often cycle in the city centre.	B: Oh, we don't.

14 Listen and check your answers.

4 Gerund or infinitive?

Complete the sentences.

1 He's afraid of *(miss)* .... his connecting flight.
2 He wouldn't like *(get)* .... another parking ticket.
3 He used *(drive)* .... to work but now he goes by bike.
4 In London most people spend a lot of time *(travel)* .... on the underground.
5 Many people still enjoy *(take)* .... the ferry when they travel to France.
6 They dislike *(use)* .... the channel tunnel, but it is faster.
7 Her parents want her *(do)* .... her driving test again.
8 She doesn't mind *(take)* .... more driving lessons.

p. 78

4 Travel

1 Holidays

When you hear the word *holiday*, which of the following words do you think of?

- relaxation
- sun and sand
- sightseeing
- cost
- long flights
- strange food

What other words and phrases come to mind? Brainstorm in class.

Now look at the *types of holiday* and the *places to stay* in the *Topic vocabulary*. Talk to your partner.

- Has he / she been on any of the types of holidays in the list? Which ones? How many times?
- Has he / she stayed in any of these places? Which ones?

→ Topic vocabulary, p. 69

remember Use the **present perfect** to talk about an action or situation which happened at some time in your life. You don't say when it happened:

- *I've been on a cruise.*

Compare:

- *I went to Berlin last year.*
- *I've been to Berlin twice.*

The present perfect is often used with **ever** and **never**:

- *I've never stayed in a youth hostel.*

→ Grammar, p. 89

2a What to say: Showing interest

Really?	Great!	Oh no!
Yes.	Sounds lovely.	How awful.
Yeah.	That's nice.	That's terrible.
Is that right?	Lucky you.	Rather you than me.

Respond to the following remarks using one of the reactions from the box. There are several possibilities for each one.

A: I've just been to Las Vegas for a week. B: ....

A: Yes. We visited a different casino every night. B: ....

A: Yes, and I lost all my money. B: ....

15 Now listen to the dialogue. How did B reply? Practise saying the dialogue with your partner. Pay attention to the intonation.

16 Listen to these short dialogues. How do the women show interest? How do the men continue?

2b Sounds lovely

First write down three or four statements (positive and negative) about your last holiday. In pairs, one student reads out his/her sentence, the other reacts, then the first student adds a sentence with further details.
Act out one of your dialogues to the class.

3 It was wonderful!

A dreadful holiday
A marvellous holiday
A bad weather holiday
A stressful holiday
A relaxing holiday
An unusual holiday

Choose one of the categories above to talk about and find three or four adjectives to describe your holiday in the *Topic vocabulary*.
Talk about your holidays in small groups. Remember to react by using some of the phrases from activity 2a. Try and ask some questions, too.

→ Topic vocabulary, p. 69

4 Different countries, different customs

Have you ever been on holiday abroad? Tell the class which countries you have visited. How many different countries has the class been to?

17 Now listen to Rob and then Sarah talking about some of the customs they encountered on holiday. Which countries did they visit?

17 Listen again and note down as many of the different customs as you can. Compare in class.

In small groups, discuss which ones you think

- are easy to get used to
- are difficult to get used to

Now tell the class if you have ever been surprised or shocked by anything you've seen abroad or by anything you've seen foreigners doing in your country?
What customs in your country might seem strange to foreigners?

5 Talking points: Travel

In groups of three, take it in turns to choose a question to ask the others. Is there a question you'd like to ask your teacher?

- Do you usually go abroad on holiday? Why? Why not?
- Do you – or would you – learn any words of the language or find out about the culture of the place you're going to visit?
- Do you usually eat the local food when you're on holiday?
- Have you seen or read about tourists behaving badly in your country or abroad?
- Have you ever been in a difficult situation abroad? Do you know someone else who has had a bad experience?
- Are there any countries you would avoid? Why?

→ L & C, p. 69

Priests blessing crowd with holy water, Lalibela, Ethiopia

Tip **Intonation**
English speakers show how interested or enthusiastic they are by using an intonation pattern that sometimes sounds exaggerated to many German speakers. But remember: If your intonation is flat, you may sound bored or impolite.

1 What to say: Reacting to what people say

18 First read the sentences below. Then listen to the reactions. Write the correct reaction under each sentence.

a) We're flying to New Zealand tomorrow.

....

b) I met someone on holiday and we're getting married.

....

c) We even went scuba-diving.

....

d) The holiday flat was filthy when we arrived.

....

e) It was dreadful. It rained all week.

....

f) Some of the villages didn't even have electricity.

....

g) Fred's broken his leg so we can't go on holiday.

....

h) There were white sandy beaches and the sea was blue.

....

19 Now listen to the mini-dialogues. Pay attention to the intonation.

2 Pronunciation

In each group there is one word in which the vowel is pronounced differently. Put a circle around the word.

1	eat	great	easy
2	good	soon	food
3	dream	dreadful	breathtaking
4	could	country	would
5	really	ideal	weather
6	one	won	on

20 Now listen to the words and check your pronunciation.

3 Find the word

Complete B's comments. Choose an adjective which has a similar meaning to the one A uses: *breathtaking, charming, dreadful, exhausting, filthy, friendly, impressive, terrified, wonderful*

1 A: It was a marvellous sightseeing holiday.
B: Yeah, it was w ....
2 A: I've never seen such magnificent buildings.
B: Neither have I – very ....
3 A: And what a picturesque fishing village!
B: Yeah, it was ...., wasn't it?
4 A: The mountain scenery was quite spectacular.
B: You're right. It was quite ....
5 A: Though, I must admit I'm afraid of heights.
B: So am I. I'm ....!
6 A: The streets in the old part of the city were so dirty.
B: Dirty! They were ....!
7 A: And I think the food was terrible.
B: Me too. It was ....
8 A: The owners at the B&B were very hospitable.
B: Yes, very .... people.
9 A: But too much sightseeing can be very tiring.
B: Yeah, quite ....

4 Been or gone?

Cross out the wrong word.

1 They've *been / gone* to Paris. They're staying at a hotel near Notre Dame.
2 We've *been / gone* abroad many times.
3 Have you ever *been / gone* to Spain?
4 I haven't seen him for a few days. I think he's *been / gone* on holiday.
5 She's *been / gone* to Minorca. That's why she's got a wonderful suntan.

p. 78

5 Looking after yourself

1 How healthy are you?

First tell the class one healthy thing you've done today and one unhealthy thing. Now put a tick (✔) in each box that applies to you.

Healthy

Do you ...

- ☐ have about 7-8 hours of sleep per night?
- ☐ eat a lot of fruit and vegetables?
- ☐ drink a lot of water?
- ☐ do energetic activity for at least 20 minutes three or four times a week?
- ☐ take opportunities for exercise, e.g. walk up stairs instead of using the lift?

Unhealthy

Do you ...

- ☐ eat too many fatty foods and/or sweet things?
- ☐ drink more than three cups of coffee per day?
- ☐ have more than two alcoholic drinks per day?
- ☐ smoke?
- ☐ do too little exercise?

First look at the first three sections of the *Topic vocabulary* for some useful words and phrases. Then in small groups, tell each other

- about the healthy and unhealthy things you've ticked and give some details
- which unhealthy things you'd like to change and which ones you don't want to (and why)

→ **Topic vocabulary, p. 70**

→ **L & C, p. 70**

remember **Much** and **many** are mostly used in questions and negatives.

- *Do you do much exercise?*
- *I don't eat many fatty things.*

They are used in positive sentences with *so* and *too*.

- *I drink too much coffee.*

In conversation, **a lot of** or **lots of** are often used in questions, negative and positive sentences.

- *I have lots of energy.*
- *I don't do a lot of exercise.*

→ **Grammar, p. 92**

2a What to say: Using question tags

Tags *(You play tennis, don't you?)* are used to ask for confirmation or agreement or to check information. They mean the same as *Is that right?* or *Do you agree?* and are often used to open a conversation or to keep the conversation going.

21 You'll hear two women having a chat at the fitness centre. Before you listen, read these sentences from the conversation and add the tags. Then listen and check your answers.

It's busy tonight, ...?

She doesn't come here very often, ...?

She's lost a lot of weight, ...?

She wasn't as thin as that before, ...?

You'll just have to do more exercise, ...?

You're not stopping already, ...?

! Note:

Positive sentence – negative tag.

Negative sentence – positive tag.

You love chocolate, don't you?

2b Is that right?

What did people say about themselves in exercise 1?
Check whether you can remember the information correctly by using tags.

! Note: If you are asking for confirmation or checking information, your voice should go down at the end of the tag. *You go to a fitness centre, don't you?*

3 Health issues

Look at the following contents page of a health magazine.

contents

September • Volume 12

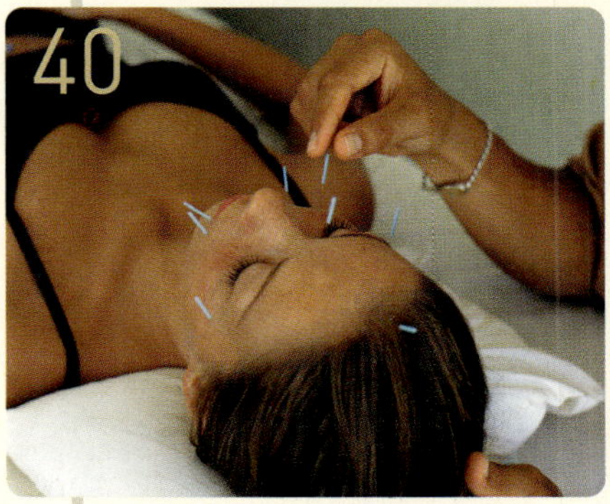

Work in small groups and tell each other
- which article(s) you would choose to read and why
- which article(s) you wouldn't want to read and why

Have you ever been on a diet?

When did you give up smoking?

Now tell each other what you know about the health issues in this contents page.
Perhaps you know some facts or can talk about your own personal experience. Ask each other questions.

4 Stress: A modern-day disease?

22 You'll hear some people talking about things that they find stressful nowadays. What things do they mention? Do these things affect you or people you know in the same way?

Here are some other things that might lead to stress. Give each one a number from 1 to 5 depending on how stressful you find them (1 = not very stressful at all, 5 = very stressful).

- ☐ Shopping
- ☐ Christmas
- ☐ Organising a holiday
- ☐ Using public transport
- ☐ Overwork
- ☐ Job insecurity
- ☐ Bringing up children
- ☐ Difficult neighbours / colleagues

Compare your numbers with another student. Try to explain why you put the numbers you did. Look at the *Topic vocabulary* for some useful adjectives to describe how you feel.

→ **Topic vocabulary, p. 70**

5 The ideal present

In pairs, decide which of the presents below you would give to each other and why. Which ones would you give to other members of your class and your teacher? Which present would you choose for yourself?

- *self-help book on stress management*
- *a book of low-cholesterol recipes*
- *a CD of relaxing music*
- *a video of yoga exercises*
- *a rowing machine*
- *a bicycle*
- *a pair of running shoes*
- *a fitness ball*
- *a variety of herbal teas*
- *a year's subscription to a fitness centre of your choice*
- *a pet*
- *free baby-sitting service for six months*
- *a voucher for a wellness weekend in a three-star hotel*
- *a six-month supply of nicotine chewing gum*

He likes jogging, doesn't he?

So how about the running shoes?

Tip **Starting a conversation**

A question tag is often used when starting a conversation with a stranger or with someone you don't know very well. A direct question can sometimes sound too abrupt or impolite. The use of the tag is a signal for the other person to react and to continue the conversation.

1 What to say: Starting a conversation with question tags

You are doing a stress management course with people you don't know very well. Here are some conversation starters. Add a tag to each one.

1 Hello, we've met before, ...?

2 Hi, I think we know each other, ...?

3 There aren't many people here, ...?

4 It's a great course, ...?

5 Jessica gave us some good tips, ...?

6 It was a good class, ...?

7 Those breathing exercises weren't easy, ...?

8 Excuse me, you don't know where I can get a cup of coffee, ...?

Here are three replies. Which reply goes with which conversation starter? Write the correct number in the box.

☐ a) Yes, of course we do. We met at Bill's party.

☐ b) Yes, it is. I think I'm really learning something useful.

☐ c) No, that's true. I'll have to practise those a few times, I think.

2a Question tags: Up or down?

When you're asking a "real" question your voice goes up at the end of the tag to show you don't know the answer.

When you're asking a question for confirmation or agreement your voice goes down.

23 Listen to the following questions and tick (✔) the two "real" questions.

1 You don't get much sleep, do you? ☐

2 You haven't cancelled your subscription, have you? ☐

3 You're here for the first time, aren't you? ☐

4 You can come, can't you? ☐

2b Pronunciation: Sounds and stress

24 Listen to the following groups of words and practise the pronunciation of the sounds in bold. Press the pause button after each group and repeat:

1 *__v__oucher, __v__ariety, __v__egetables*

1 **v**oucher	**v**ariety	**v**egetables
2 **ch**ocolate	**Ch**inese	**ch**ewing gum
3 **ch**olesterol	**Ch**ristmas	al**c**oholic
4 **c**omprehensive	**c**onscious	**c**onvenience
5 re**c**ipe	**s**ub**s**cription	in**s**omnia
6 homeopa**th**ic	heal**th**y	aroma**th**erapy

24 Now listen to the words again and underline the part of the word where the main stress falls like this: *voucher*. Check your answers in the *Key*.

3 Find the right verb

John is talking about his friend Mary. Read what he says and complete the phrases with the right form of the following verbs: *be, bring up, go on, eat, exercise, give up, live, lose, suffer from*

Mary is a single mum and has to (1) .... her two children on her own. When she (2) .... too much stress, she (3) .... lots of junk food and is now seriously overweight. But she really wants (4) .... a healthier life. She plans (5) .... regularly and her doctor has told her (6) .... a strict diet so she soon hopes (7) .... weight. She also wants (8) .... smoking because she (9) .... often short of breath.

p. 78

6 Free time

1 Your main occupation

What is your main occupation: working? studying? looking after your home or family? looking for a new job? How many hours a day are taken up by this? Tell the class.

2 What do you do in your free time?

What do you do with the rest of your time? Look at the following activities. If you do anything else, write it in an empty space. There are some more activities in the *Topic vocabulary*. → Topic vocabulary, p. 71

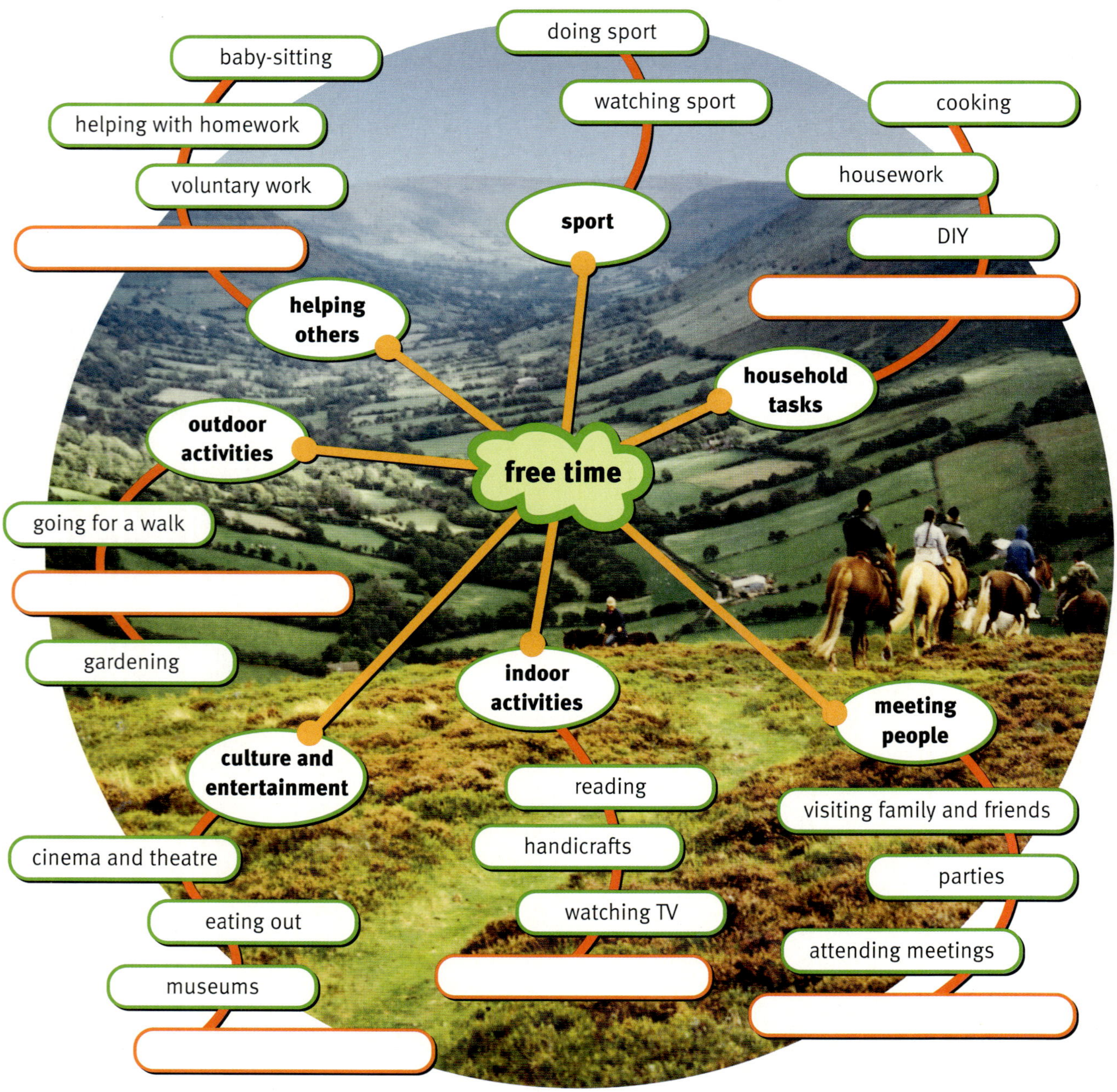

In pairs, find the following:

- two activities you both do regularly
- one activity you both do now and again
- an activity you both think you should spend more time doing
- an activity you'd both like to spend more time doing
- an activity you both really enjoy
- an activity you both dislike

→ L & C, p. 71

3 What to say: Giving yourself more time

In everyday conversation, people often use fillers such as *um, mm, well, you know* to give themselves more time to think. The phrases in the box below can have the same function.

- ☐ Just one moment.
- ☐ Let me think.
- ☐ Wait, that's not all.
- ☐ There's more.
- ☐ Sorry, I haven't quite finished.

25 You'll hear two people answering questions about their interests. What do they say?

25 Listen carefully to how the speakers give themselves time. Tick (✔) the phrases in the box that the speakers use.

4a Interests

Have you got one or more interests or hobbies that are important to you? Or did you use to have one that you don't do anymore?

First look at the *Useful phrases* in the *Topic vocabulary* and then tell your partner what you are / used to be interested in.

Here are two questions you could ask about one of your partner's interests. Add four questions of your own.

1 How much time do / did you spend doing it?
2 How did you become interested in it?
3 ....
4 ....
5 ....
6 ....

Take it in turns to ask and answer questions. Try and use some of the phrases from activity 3.

→ Topic vocabulary, p. 71

Bob Lerch, collector of Bakelite objects, listens to one of his many Bakelite radios. Bakelite was a revolutionary plastic popular between the 1920s and the 1940s.

4a Further ideas:

- playing an instrument
- canoeing
- voluntary work
- handicrafts and DIY
- gardening
- theatre, cinema
- painting

4b Who has got the most unusual interest?

Write down three things you need(ed) for one of your interests and one adjective that describes it. The adjectives in the *Topic vocabulary* might help you. If you're not sure of the word in English, ask your teacher or look in a dictionary.

water, life jacket, paddle, peaceful.

Read out one of your words to the class. Can the others guess what you like(d) doing? Continue reading out your words until the others have guessed correctly.

remember **Comparatives and superlatives**

Use **–er** and **–est** for one-syllable and some two-syllable adjectives:
- *It's cheaper than going to the opera.*
- *She's got the healthiest pastime.*

Use **more** and **most** with some two-syllable and three-syllable adjectives:
- *It's more relaxing than playing football.*
- *It's the most active sport.*

Here are some other ways of comparing:
- *It's (not) as dangerous as windsurfing.*
- *It's less expensive than collecting antiques.*

→ **Grammar, p. 92**

In small groups, decide which hobby or interest in your class is:

	Hobby / Interest	Name of student
the most expensive?	....	....
the most active?	....	....
the most unusual?	....	....
the most relaxing?	....	....
the least dangerous?	....	....
requires the most skill?	....	....

Compare in class. Do you agree? Has someone got an interest that you would like to take up? Which one?

5 How do you unwind?

People have different ways of unwinding after a stressful day. Look at the photos. Do you like doing these things?

26 Now listen to some people saying what they do to relax and note down the things they mention. Compare your answers with a partner and then in class.

Work in small groups and tell each other
- if you enjoy or would enjoy doing any of the things mentioned
- how you unwind after a stressful day
- if you feel guilty about taking time off to relax

6 Choices

Talk in small groups. Would you prefer:

more free time	or	more money
more time alone	or	more time with other people
more labour-saving devices	or	more time to cook and clean
more things to do in your free time	or	fewer things to do in your free time
an active hobby	or	a relaxing one

Give some reasons for your choices.
If you had a free choice to spend your weekend as you want, what would you do? What are you going to do?

> **Tip** **Apologising for interrupting**
> In Unit 6 activity 3 the woman in the first dialogue used the phrase *Sorry. Carry on.* when she wanted to apologize for interrupting. Here are some more phrases you could use:
> *Sorry. Do go on.*
> *Please continue.*
> *Sorry, you were saying?*

1 What to say: Apologising

Fill in two ways A can apologise for interrupting:

A: How do you unwind?
B: Let me think. Well, I often phone a friend for a nice long chat.
A: So do I, but what ...?
B: Wait, that's not all.
A: Sorry, y............. w............... s................ (1)?
Sorry, p..................... c........................... (2).
B: Yeah, and I sometimes spend an hour or two playing video games.

Now fill in two more ways B can apologise:

A: How do I unwind? Well, I enjoy a long soak in the bath.
B: Me too. And what about your partner?
A: One moment, I haven't quite finished.
B: Oh s.................... . C................. o........... (3).
S.................. . D.......... g.......... o.......... (4).

2 Pronunciation: The sound [ə]

You saw in Unit 1 that [ə] is used very often in English. Some very common words in English (*was, of, at, than*, etc.) are often pronounced with the unstressed [ə] sound in sentences. Your English will sound more natural if you use it.

27 Listen to the pronunciation of *to, was, than* in the following sentences. You will hear each sentence twice. Tick (✔) the box when you hear the [ə].

	1	2
a) I walk to the gym.	☐	☐
b) He was in the swimming pool.	☐	☐
c) It's more expensive than mine.	☐	☐

Now underline the [ə] sounds in these sentences.

1 Let's go for a walk. (2 sounds)
2 How about a glass of wine? (3 sounds)
3 It's as good as mine. (2 sounds)
4 He goes to church regularly. (2 sounds)
5 When he was a young man he played in a band. (3 sounds)
6 Jogging can be more tiring than swimming. (2 sounds)

Check your answers in the *Key*.

28 Now listen to the sentences again and repeat.

3 Some good advice

At a weekend seminar on stress management one of the speakers gives some useful tips on how to make the best use of one's free time. Fill in the missing words: *about, at* (x4), *for, in, of, off* (x2), *on* (2x) *up*

1 After a hard day .... the office, put .... your running shoes and go .... a jog.
2 If you're not keen .... being active, just listen to some music and switch ....
3 Don't feel guilty .... taking time .... to relax.
4 Just walking around the garden is another good way .... unwinding.
5 Do a course .... evening school if you're not good .... DIY. It's very useful.
6 If you are bad .... remembering facts, you should train your memory.
7 Why don't you take .... golf if you want to enjoy plenty of fresh air and exercise.
8 If you're interested .... collecting antiques, look up the offers on the Internet.

p. 78

Extra 1

Wales

1 Quiz

Wales is part of the United Kingdom – a country which is only 60 miles wide (96 km) and 160 miles long (257 km), but it is a country which is very different from England, Scotland and Northern Ireland because of its history, language and traditions.

Test your knowledge on Wales by completing the quiz.

Tick (✔) the correct answer.

1 The number of inhabitants in Wales is
O 1 million O 2.9 million O 4 million

2 The capital of Wales is
O Swansea O Caernarfon O Cardiff

3 The highest mountain in Wales is
O Snowdon O Ben Nevis O Sugar Loaf

4 A referendum for a democratic Welsh assembly was held in
O 1918 O 1950 O 1997

5 The day-to-day language for most people today is
O English O Welsh O Erse

6 The percentage of people in Wales who speak Welsh is
O 50% O 20% O 1.9%

7 Welsh has been compulsory in schools since
O 1900 O 1951 O 1998

8 There is a long-established Welsh-speaking community in
O Greece O Patagonia O Italy

9 Which flower is one of the national emblems of Wales?
O rose O daffodil O thistle

10 And which animal?
O dragon O sheep O bull

11 The most popular sport is
O cricket O baseball O rugby

12 Who is the famous Welsh star?
O Tom Jones O Elton John O Sean Connery

13 The first English Prince of Wales was born in Caernarfon in
O 1284 O 1536 O 1800

14 Charles Windsor officially became Prince of Wales in
O 1948 O 1969 O 1981

Compare your answers with a partner. Talk about the answers which are different. The following phrases will be useful.

- *It must be ...*
- *I think ...*
- *It's definitely ...*
- *It's probably ...*

Then check the answers in the *Key*.

p. 80

Catherine Zeta-Jones, Welsh actress

Anthony Hopkins, Welsh actor

Welsh

29 Listen to these Welsh words and phrases.

Cymru — Wales
Bore da — Good morning
Sut ydych chwi? — How are you?
Da iawn, diolch — Very well, thank you
Os gwelwch yn dda — Please

Traditional dance at the Eisteddfod

2 A Week in Wales

30 Listen to David and his American friend Josh talking about David's proposed trip to Wales. Write down four things that Josh learns from David about the Welsh and Wales. Then in groups of four compare your answers.

30 Listen again and write down some phrases Josh uses to:

1 open the conversation
2 keep the conversation going
3 close the conversation

Tell the class

- something you already knew about Wales or the Welsh
- something you didn't know
- something which surprised or particularly interested you

p. 80

3 A trip to Wales

First look at the different things to do and visit in Wales and decide which things would appeal to you.

Castles on the north Wales coast

Eight massive fortresses were built in the 13th century by England's King Edward I (1230-1307) to strengthen England's control of North Wales. Each castle is unique in its own way. There are three fine examples in North Wales. In the far north lies Conway Castle, one of the most impressive in medieval Europe with a wall around the castle and the town. Then about 40 miles further south Caernarfon Castle is well worth a visit. It is a magnificently preserved castle, where the first English Prince of Wales was born. Then last but not least, you can visit the impressive ruins of the castle at Harlech, which is on the edge of a steep cliff. From the castle there are spectacular views of Snowdonia, Tremadoc Bay and the mountains to the south.

Snowdonia National Park

Have a taste of wild, romantic countryside and escape from the crowds. You can drive for miles through this breathtaking, unspoilt countryside without passing another car. The national parklands are rich in forests, moorlands, lakes, waterfalls and a magnificent wild stretch of coastline. There are numerous walks and climbs up to the summit of Snowdon. Some are steeper than others and need climbing experience. Remember there can be snow at all times of the year so choose your route carefully. There is, of course, for the less adventurous, a railway line from the village of Llanberis to the summit.

Cardiff

The city has a lot to offer the leisure visitor, with many attractions and entertainment within the city itself, and beautiful countryside and coastline just a short drive away.
Places to visit:
Cardiff Castle in a lovely park in the centre of Cardiff.
The ***National Museum*** and Gallery with its fine collection of Impressionist paintings.
The ***open-air Museum*** of Welsh life, St Fagan's with over 30 original buildings moved from

Caernarfon Castle

various parts of Wales to show how the people of Wales have lived, worked and spent their leisure time over the last five hundred years.
The ***New Theatre***, home to the Welsh Opera, but also presents ballet, drama and musical theatre.

Rhondda Heritage Park and Big Pit at Blaenafon

Take a journey through Wales' coal-mining history. Spend a few hours at the Rhondda Heritage Park, situated near Pontypridd in the Rhondda valley. At the Visitor Centre you can watch "Black Gold – The Story of Coal", an

Snowdonia National Park

audio-visual presentation of the life of the people in the Rhondda. Then put on a helmet, ride "the cage" to the pit bottom and experience what life was like for men working down the coal mines in the 1950s. If you want to go down a really old mine, you can go to Big Pit in Blaenafon, which was the place of work for hundreds of men, women and children for over 200 years. Take a walk through the town of Blaenafon itself, where the 18th century ironworks, the old houses, church and schools, and typical Welsh chapels are living images of more than two centuries of industrial history.

Pembrokeshire

The coastline of Pembrokeshire (Dyfed) in South West Wales is some of the most spectacular in Britain. There are steep sea cliffs and beautiful wide sandy bays, but also a lot of small, sheltered

Cardiff

beaches for those who like to be alone. For the active, there are magnificent walks along the cliffs, boating and sailing, water-skiing, trout and salmon angling and sea fishing. You can visit the many picturesque ports, historic towns and villages with their impressive castle ruins and, if there's time, Britain's smallest cathedral city, named after St David, patron saint of Wales. Half a mile off the coast from St David's is Ramsey island, which is a breeding ground for rare Atlantic grey seals and more than 30 species of sea birds. ■

Rhondda

Work in groups of four. You'd like to spend a week in Wales. Decide on some of the things you'd like to do together. Discuss the best way to get to Wales and talk about how you would prefer to travel once you are there: by plane, by ferry, by car, by train or on a coach with a guided tour? Report back to the class.

Pembrokeshire

4 Over to you

Work in small groups.

1 When visitors come to stay with you in your country, what places do you take them to?

2 What do you know about Wales? Discuss it in your group and then tell the class what you know or ask a question about something you would like to know.

7 Places to live

1 Different places

Take a few minutes to try and fill in as many of the following gaps as possible with the names of towns, villages, areas, etc.

.... is one of my favourite places.

.... is a place I'd really like to visit.

.... pleasantly surprised me.

.... disappointed me.

.... is a place I'd like to forget.

.... is a place which is / was important to me.

First look at the *Topic vocabulary* for some useful words and phrases. Then exchange books with a partner and find out more about some of the places your partner has written down.

- *Where is ...?*
- *What's it like?*
- *Tell me more about ... .*
- *Great!*
- *Sounds awful!*

→ Topic vocabulary, p. 72

2a Interesting places to live

	Tromsø, Norway	Alice Springs	Los Angeles
population	51,600	26,400	3,900,000
average summer temperature	11º	35º	24º
average winter temperature	-3º	20º	15º

What do you know about the following places? Tell the class.

Tromsø Alice Springs Los Angeles

31 Listen to the people talking about life in these places and note down anything you would like about living in each place. Listen again and make notes on the things you would dislike.

Alice Springs

Tromsø, Norway

2b Moving abroad

Work in small groups. Imagine that the firm you are working for is going to senc you abroad for two years with your immediate family to one of the three places mentioned in activity 2a. Which of these places

- would you absolutely refuse to live in?
- might you consider living in?
- would you like to live in?

Talk about why you would or wouldn't go there, the difficulties you might have, how the climate / living conditions would affect you.
Which is the most and the least popular place in your class?

Would you ever consider going to live in another country? Why? Why not? Which country do you think you could live in? Tell the class.

Los Angeles

3a What to say: Giving opinions

32 You'll hear three people discussing the places where they live. Which of the following subjects do they talk about? Number them in the order you hear them.

- ☐ travelling by train
- ☐ travelling by bus
- ☐ new shops
- ☐ new flats and houses
- ☐ nursery school places
- ☐ nursing home places

Look at the phrases below.

32 Listen to the exchanges again. Which two phrases aren't used?

Expressing Opinions
I think ...
If you ask me, ...
Well, personally, ...
....

Agreeing
Yes, I agree with you there.
I think you're right.
That's true.
Absolutely!
....

Disagreeing
Oh, do you think so?
I'm afraid I don't agree with you there.
Yes, but ...
....

Perhaps you know some more phrases for giving opinions or agreeing and disagreeing. Add them to the lists.

3b What about you?

Work in small groups. Take it in turns to give your opinions on an aspect of the city / town / village / area where you live. The others should agree or disagree. You could talk about some of the following:

- the public transport system
- life for families with children
- the price of houses / flats
- the cultural activities
- the nightlife
- the shops

4 Where would you like to live?

Here is a list of factors which people might consider when deciding where to buy a house or rent a flat. How important is each factor for you? Tick (✔) the appropriate box.

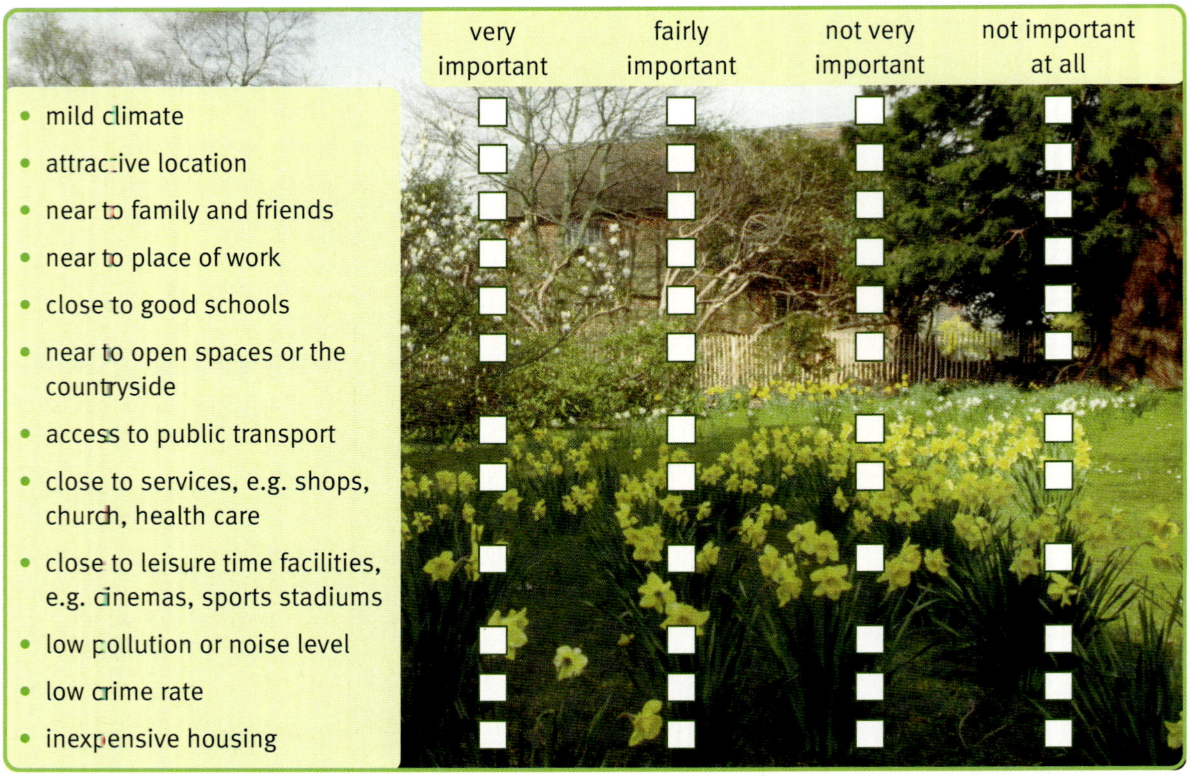

	very important	fairly important	not very important	not important at all
• mild climate	☐	☐	☐	☐
• attractive location	☐	☐	☐	☐
• near to family and friends	☐	☐	☐	☐
• near to place of work	☐	☐	☐	☐
• close to good schools	☐	☐	☐	☐
• near to open spaces or the countryside	☐	☐	☐	☐
• access to public transport	☐	☐	☐	☐
• close to services, e.g. shops, church, health care	☐	☐	☐	☐
• close to leisure time facilities, e.g. cinemas, sports stadiums	☐	☐	☐	☐
• low pollution or noise level	☐	☐	☐	☐
• low crime rate	☐	☐	☐	☐
• inexpensive housing	☐	☐	☐	☐

In pairs, compare your answers and give reasons why you answered as you did. Is there anything else which you think is important?
What are the advantages and disadvantages of the place where you now live?

5 Moving house

Tick (✔) any of the following sentences that are true for you.

- ☐ I've been living in my present house / flat for more than 10 years.
- ☐ I've moved several times.
- ☐ I still live in the town / area where I was born.
- ☐ I don't like living in one place for too long.
- ☐ I'd like to move back to the place where I grew up.
- ☐ I wouldn't mind moving to another town.
- ☐ I'd like to move into the country.
- ☐ I'd move to another place if I were offered a better paid job.
- ☐ I never want to move again.

Work in small groups. Take it in turns to give some extra information about the sentences you have ticked.

→ L & C, p. 72

Tell the class which places you have lived in.
How many different places has the class lived in?

remember

Use the **present perfect progressive** to ask or say **how long** something has been happening (up to now):

- *I've been living here for two years.*
- *How long have you been living there?*

Since and **for**:

- *I've been working there*
  since January.
  for ten months.

→ Grammar, p. 90

1 What to say: What can you say?

How could you react to the following statements about London? Two reactions are possible. Cross out the wrong one.

1 Well, personally, I think London's just a great place to live.
a) I quite agree with you. b) So do I. c) No, that's true.
2 Yes, but the traffic is a nightmare.
a) Do you think so? b) Oh, I don't. c) Yes, you're right.
3 You know, my sister had four car accidents last year.
a) That's terrible. b) I'm sorry to hear that. c) Neither did I.
4 There are lots of things to do here in London though, aren't there?
a) Yes, there certainly are. b) Yes, that's true. c) Yes, it is.
5 I read somewhere that there are 159 theatres in London.
a) Is that right? b) No, not really. c) 159?
6 And I've got tickets for the ballet next week.
a) Absolutely! b) Lucky you. c) Really? Have you?

Tip Agreeing and disagreeing

English speakers usually express their disagreement fairly mildly *(I'm afraid I ..., Yes, but ...)* because they don't want to sound too abrupt even with people they know quite well. But, in contrast, when they want to show complete agreement, they often exaggerate: *Oh, yes, absolutely. I think it's a great idea* or *I quite agree with you.*

2 Pronunciation: Certain stressed words

Some words like *very, so, rather* are often stressed in sentences to show how strongly you feel about something.

33 Listen to these six sentences and write down the stressed word in each sentence.

1 .... 3 .... 5 ....

2 .... 4 .... 6 ....

33 Now listen again and repeat what you hear. Don't be afraid to exaggerate. It will make your English sound more authentic!

3 Giving opinions

Two neighbours are talking about the new housing estate they have moved to. Write these sentences in the correct order.

1 people / are / the / personally, / nice. / **Well,** / very / I think

....

2 just / are / great. / **And** / shops / the ....

3 too. / quite / is / school / the / good, / local / **I think** ....

4 **If** / you / are / here. / ask / kids / me, / happier / the / much

....

Now match each of the following reactions to one of the opinions above. Write the correct sentence number in the box.

☐ a) Yes, that's true. Very much happier.
☐ b) Do you really think so? An awful lot of lessons are cancelled, you know.
☐ c) Yes, but they're always crowded on Saturdays.
☐ d) Absolutely! Everyone's really very friendly.

4 Vocabulary: Which words go together?

1 major	6 low	☐ a) spaces	1 f) road
2 leisure time	7 open	☐ b) school	☐ g) centre
3 town	8 pleasantly	☐ c) home	☐ h) climate
4 mild	9 nursing	☐ d) surprised	☐ i) crime rate
5 nursery		☐ e) facilities	

p. 78

8 Living with gadgets

1 How do you communicate?

Look at the photos of different methods of communication. Which ones have you used, sent or received today? Tell the class.

Now order the following according to how often you use them to communicate with other people.
Put a number 1 in the method you use most often and so on. Put a cross in those you never use.

- ☐ e-mail
- ☐ Internet, e.g. chatrooms, booking travel, online banking
- ☐ Fax
- ☐ telephone
- ☐ mobile phone
- ☐ text messaging
- ☐ handwritten letters
- ☐ postcards
- ☐ greetings cards
- ☐ other: please state

……………………………………………

……………………………………………

First look at the first three sections of the *Topic vocabulary* to remind you of some useful words and phrases. Then compare your order with a partner and

- give some details about how often / when you use each method.
- say which method you enjoy / don't enjoy using. Why?
- say if your order would have been the same five years ago and if you think your order will change in the future. Why?

Remember to react to your partner's statements.

So do I. *Neither did I.* *Oh, I don't.*

→ Topic vocabulary, p. 73
→ L & C, p. 73

2 What to say: Describing things

34 You will hear students describing five objects they don't know the names of in English. Write down what you think they're describing. You'll find all five objects in the list of *Useful gadgets* in the *Topic vocabulary*. Compare your answers in class.

It's (flat, round, small, large).
It's made of (plastic, metal).
It's sort of (square, heavy).
It's something / a thing that (heats a room).
(that) (you use for shaving).
with (a handle on the top).
It's a sort of (box).
It's used for (cook)ing.
(It copies, prints) and things.

In pairs, take it in turns to describe a gadget you have at home or at work or choose one or more from the *Topic vocabulary*. Use some of the phrases from the box. Can your partner guess what it is?

→ Topic vocabulary, p. 73

"For heaven's sake, Colin! Just pass me the ketchup."

3 Everyday devices

Make a list of the electric and electronic devices that you used yesterday or have used today – at home, at work or elsewhere. If you don't know the word, try and describe it using some of the phrases from activity 2.

Work in small groups. Tell each other what devices you have used and give some details (Why did you use it? Where?).

Have you got any gadgets at home or at work that you never use? Tell your group about them.

4 It doesn't work!

35 You'll hear some people talking about things that have broken down or don't work any longer. Listen and note down what happened to each of the things that are mentioned. Compare your answers with a partner and then in class.

You want to tell the others about a thing or things at home or at work that broke down. Think about what was wrong with it, how you dealt with it, how it affected your life / routine. Note down some of the words and phrases you might need. Ask your teacher or look in a dictionary or *Topic vocabulary* for help with unknown vocabulary.

→ **Topic vocabulary, p. 73**

In small groups, take it in turns to tell each other your "breakdown" stories.

What was wrong with it?

Oh no!

That's terrible.

5 A final word

Work in small groups. Name two or three gadgets and devices

- you would find it difficult to live without and why
- you sometimes find annoying and why
- you'd like to buy in the future and why
- you didn't use to have and how you managed without them

remember

Use **used to** to say that something happened regularly in the past, or was true in the past, but is different now:

- *I used to send my letters by post.*
- *We used to have a black and white television.*
- *We didn't use to watch TV much.*

→ **Grammar, p. 93**

Tip **It's a thingy.**

In everyday conversation when you cannot remember a word or do not know the word or name for an object, you can always use words like *thingy, thingummy, thingamajig, thingamabob* or *what-d'you-call-it*. Which word do you like the best? Choose one to learn.

1 What to say: Describing things

Fill in the missing words using some of the phrases from activity 2.

1 Can you pass me the thingamagig? That black thing you u __ __ __ __ __ opening tins.

2 What's that thingamabob? Is it a s __ __ __ __ __ thermostat?

3 It's u __ __ __ __ __ __ making holes in the wall. You know an electric thingy.

4 It's a what-d'you-call-it - something t __ __ __ heats a room.

5 That's an interesting-looking thingummy. Is it m __ __ __ __ __ plastic?

6 Oh, what's it called? It's black, f __ __ __ and s __ __ __ __ __ __ and you use it in your computer.

Now write down the two objects they are describing in numbers 3 and 6:

....

2 Pronunciation: [s] or [z]

Look at the following sentences and underline each "s" which is pronounced with a voiced [z]. Do it like this: *I always send postcards*. Then check your answers in the *Key*.

1 That wasn't such a useful device after all.
2 It's used for sending messages.
3 He didn't use to use the phone so much.
4 It's something he doesn't often use.
5 This old cell phone of yours isn't much use.

36 Listen to the sentences and pay attention to the voiced [z].

36 Then listen again and repeat the sentences. Be careful: each "s" which is not underlined is pronounced with a voiceless [s].

3 Vocabulary: faulty equipment

Two friends are talking about some technical problems. Complete B's answers. Look at the section on *Technical breakdown* in your *Topic vocabulary* if you need help.

A: My car isn't working.
B: Has it broken .... (1) altogether?

A: It just won't start.
B: Perhaps there's something .... (2) with the electrics.

A: And my fax machine's out of order, too.
B: Yes, it was making .... (3) yesterday.

A: Yes, it doesn't seem to work at all.
B: Perhaps there's an electrical .... (4).

4 What can you say?

Two words are correct. Cross out the wrong word.

Peter had a stressful day at work.

1 He made several *town* / *long-distance* / *local* calls.
2 He *got* / *became* / *sent* dozens of e-mails.
3 He *ordered* / *cancelled* / *booked* his flight to New York.
4 He *lost* / *deleted* / *left* a very important file when his computer crashed.
5 He asked a technician to come and *look at* / *look for* / *mend* his scanner.

p. 79

9 Money matters

1 You and your money

Work in pairs. **Student A**: Ask the first question. Then follow the arrows depending on whether your partner answers *yes* or *no*. **Student B**: Answer each question with *yes* or *no* and add a few details. Now change roles.

Yes, I do actually. I … *No, as a matter of fact I wouldn't. I …*

Start here

- *Do you often worry about how much money you're spending?* — **Yes** → Do you always look at the price of food items …? / **No** → Do you often compare prices …?
- *Do you often compare prices before you buy non-food items?* — **Yes** → Do you always look at the price of food items …? / **No** → Do you often go into a shop …?
- *Do you often go into a shop for one thing and come out with two or three extras?* — **Yes** → Would you buy shares? / **No** → Do you usually check your change …?
- *Do you always look at the price of food items before you put them into your shopping trolley?* — **Yes** → Do you keep a record …? / **No** → Do you usually check your change …?
- *Do you usually check your change in shops when you pay cash?* — **Yes** → Do you keep a record …? / **No** → Do you know how much money …?
- *Would you buy shares?* — **Yes** → Would you go to a casino …? / **No** → Do you know how much money …?
- *Do you keep a record of how much money you spend?* — **Yes** → Do you often feel guilty …? / **No** → Do you know how much money …?
- *Do you know how much money you've got on you at the moment?* — **Yes** → Do you often feel guilty …? / **No** → Would you go to a casino …?
- *Would you go to a casino and try your luck?* — **Yes** → Do you often go on a spending spree? / **No** → Would you take out a large bank loan …?
- *Do you often feel guilty when you buy things on impulse?* — **Yes** → You are extremely careful … / **No** → Would you take out a large bank loan …?
- *Would you take out a large bank loan to buy a house or flat or start a business?* — **Yes** → Do you often go on a spending spree? / **No** → You're good at looking after your money …
- *Do you often go on a spending spree?* — **Yes** → Your bank balance … / **No** → You're good at looking after your money …

You are extremely careful with money. Your bank manager probably likes you, too!

You're good at looking after your money. But why don't you take a risk now and again?

Your bank balance probably doesn't look too healthy but at least you're having fun.

2 What to say: Giving longer answers

37 Listen to the differences between the following exchanges.

Your conversation will be more successful
- if you show that you are interested
- if you give extra information and add comments to your answers whenever possible

How might you answer the questions on the recording? Compare your ideas in class.

Take it in turns to ask your partner those questions from activity 1 he/she didn't answer. Your partner should try and give as much extra information as possible.

Shopping mall in Las Vegas

3a Shopping in the States

What do you know about shopping in the USA? Tell the class.

Pamela, an American woman, is being interviewed by someone doing some market research on shopping habits. Before you listen, match the American words with the British words and compare your answers in class.

1	store	a)	☐	city centre
2	mall	b)	☐	trolley
3	convenience store	c)	☐	chemist's
4	pharmacy	d)	☐	shop
5	downtown	e)	☐	handbag
6	parking lot	f)	☐	trousers
7	pants	g)	☐	shopping centre
8	cart	h)	☐	banknote
9	bill	i)	☐	corner shop
10	purse	j)	☐	car park

38 Now listen to some of Pamela's answers. Write down the seven questions you think she was asked. Compare in class. Think of another question the interviewer could ask.

38 Listen again. Did Pamela mention anything about shopping in the USA that you really liked / didn't like? Why? Tell the class.

→ L & C, p. 74

3b Your shopping habits

You are going to answer the questions you wrote down in activity 3a. Look at the *Topic vocabulary* and find four or five words or phrases that you think you might use in your answers.

Work in pairs. Ask each other the questions and find out as much as possible about your partner's shopping habits. Remember to show interest and encourage your partner to say more.

Me too. *Really?* *Yeah.* *So, what do you ...?*

Could you go shopping with your partner? Tell the class why or why not.

→ Topic vocabulary, p. 74

4a Spending money

Write down two or three things you're planning to buy in the next six months.

pair of shoes
jewellery
bottle of Schnapps

washing machine
bicycle

Work in groups of four. Take it in turns to say one thing you're going to buy. If possible, the others should give you some advice on where you should or should not buy it and why.

Why don't you ...?
I (don't) think you should ...,
I wouldn't go to ... because ...,
Don't go to ... because ...

Tell the class one thing you've decided to buy and where you're (not) going to buy it.

remember Use **going to** to say what you have already decided to do or are planning to do in the future:

- *I'm going to buy a necklace for my wife.*
- *I'm not going to buy it at the jeweller's on the main street.*

→ Grammar, p. 91

4b How to save money

Here is part of a leaflet that gives tips on how to save money.

Work in groups of three. Which of the things on the list

- do you do?
- do you think are a good idea?
- do you think are a bad idea?

In your groups think of some other ways of saving money. Then compare your ideas in class.

If you ask me, ...
Personally, I think ...

100 ways to save

- Use your bike more and save on petrol
- Stop buying lottery tickets
- Only eat out on special occasions
- Take your own snacks when travelling
- Look on the Internet for bargain holidays and cheap flights
- Only use your mobile for emergencies
- Start using cheap telephone numbers
- Make a shopping list and only buy what's on it
- Buy things second-hand at flea markets or on eBay
- Look for special offers or buy two for the price of one

Tip **One-word answers**

Answering with just *yes* or *no* can often sound impolite or unfriendly if you are talking to someone you don't know very well. In activity 1 you learnt the phrases: *Yes, actually I do / I would*, etc. *No, as a matter of fact I don't / haven't*, etc. Here are some more ways English speakers avoid using one-word answers:
Yes, certainly / of course.
Yes, that's right.
Yes, I think so.
No, I'm afraid I don't / haven't, etc.
No, that's true.
No, I don't think so.

1 What to say: Giving more information

Two people (A and B) are having a chat on the bus. Here are some questions they ask.

A: Hello, you've got a lot of bags. Have you been to the new shopping mall? B: ☐
A: Did you like it then? B: ☐
A: It's a bit crowded though, isn't it? B: ☐
A: Have you finished your Christmas shopping then? B: ☐

B: Do you know what I could buy for a 16-year-old boy? A: ☐
B: Ah, this is our stop. Could you help me with my bags? A: ☐
B: Oh no, I've forgotten to buy some bread. Is there a food shop near here? A: ☐

Match these answers to the questions above. Write the correct number in the box.

1 Yes, that's true. Especially just before Christmas.
2 Yes, I have. I've just spent all day there.
3 Yes, of course. Let me take this one.
4 Well, yes, as a matter of fact I did. I loved it. I found some great bargains.
5 No, I don't think so but there's one on the main road.
6 No, actually I haven't. I still need to buy a present for my son.
7 No, I'm afraid I don't. My boys are still at nursery school.

2 Pronunciation: Asking questions

When you ask questions with a question word like *what* or *how*, your voice normally goes down at the end of the sentence. ↘
When there is no question word, your voice goes up. ↗

Look at the following questions. Put a ↘ or a ↗ in each box.

1 ☐ Why don't you invest some money in shares?
2 ☐ Would you want to take out a bank loan?
3 ☐ Have you asked your bank manager ?
4 ☐ Which shares would you consider buying?
5 ☐ Do you worry about borrowing money?
6 ☐ When did you last check your bank balance?

Check your answers in the *Key*.

39 Now listen to the sentences and repeat.

3 Vocabulary: Find the word

Pamela's girlfriend is asking her about her recent trip to the newly opened shopping mall. Complete the phrases with the following words: *assistants, bargains, choice, fun, offers, prices, quality, service, trip, value*

1 A: Did you enjoy your shopping ....?
B: Yes, I did. It was a lot of ....

2 A: What's the customer .... like?
B: Excellent. The shop .... are very friendly.

3 A: Are the .... reasonable?
B: Yes, they are. You get good .... for money.

4 A: Is there a wide ....?
B: Yeah, and the .... isn't bad either.

5 A: Did you buy any special ....?
B: Well, not this time. There were no real ....

p. 79

10 Fears and challenges

1a Fears and phobias

Did you know?

- Singer **Aretha Franklin** is **terrified of flying**. She doesn't travel on planes, even for concerts on the other side of the country.
- **Napoleon Buonaparte**, **Julius Caesar** and **Benito Mussolini** were all **frightened of cats**.
- Film director **Alfred Hitchcock** was **afraid of eggs**.
- **Elizabeth I of England** suffered from **anthophobia**, a fear of roses.
- **Howard Hughes**, the millionaire, had a **fear of germs**. He went through four boxes of tissues a day, wiping off everything he came into contact with.

Which other famous people have a fear or phobia? Do you know anyone or have you heard about anyone who has a fear or phobia? Tell the class about it.

1b How brave are you?

Look at the following situations and put a circle round a number for each one depending on how frightened you would be.

	calm	slightly uneasy	nervous	very nervous	afraid	very frightened	terrified
Seeing a mouse in the kitchen	1	2	3	4	5	6	7
Finding a large spider in the bath	1	2	3	4	5	6	7
Flying in a plane	1	2	3	4	5	6	7
Going to the dentist	1	2	3	4	5	6	7
Being stuck in a tunnel / a lift	1	2	3	4	5	6	7
Being outside in a thunderstorm	1	2	3	4	5	6	7
Being on top of a high building	1	2	3	4	5	6	7
Being home alone at night	1	2	3	4	5	6	7

First look at the first two sections of the *Topic vocabulary* for some useful adjectives and phrases. Then in small groups, compare your answers. Is there anything all of you are a little scared of? Is there anything that nobody finds at all scary?

Then find out from the people in your group

- if there is a reason why they are afraid of these things
- if there is anything else that makes them feel nervous
- how it affects them

Try and give some extra information whenever possible.

→ Topic vocabulary, p. 75

1b

Further ideas:
- dogs
- injections
- crowded places
- wasps
- meeting strangers
- water
- exams

2a Scary moments

40/41 You'll hear two people talking about a frightening experience they've had. Listen and write down what they were scared of.

How do you think you would feel in either of these situations? Tell the class.

40/41 Listen again and put a tick (✔) in the correct column.

Who	The woman	The man
started sweating?	☐	☐
was a bit short of breath?	☐	☐
had butterflies in his / her stomach?	☐	☐
felt faint?	☐	☐
fainted?	☐	☐

Whose	The woman's	The man's
voice was shaking?	☐	☐
heart beat faster?	☐	☐
legs were shaking?	☐	☐

2b What to say: Structuring a conversation

41 Listen again to the man describing his parachute jump. He uses six of the following expressions. Tick (✔) the ones you hear. Which one isn't used?

- ☐ At first
- ☐ Then
- ☐ After that
- ☐ In the end
- ☐ You'll never guess what happened
- ☐ Suddenly
- ☐ And the next thing I knew

In pairs, take it in turns to retell the story, with each student saying one sentence at a time. Try and use some of the phrases from the box.

2c Your story

You are going to tell each other about one or more experiences that made you (or someone you know) feel nervous or frightened. Think about what happened, how you felt and how it turned out in the end. Look at the *Topic vocabulary* for some useful phrases.

In groups of three, tell each other about your experiences. Use some of the phrases from activity 2b. Ask your teacher about one of his / her frightening experiences.

→ Topic vocabulary, p. 75

2c Further ideas:
- a job interview
- an oral exam
- a medical examination
- an accident
- losing your way
- speaking a foreign language

3 Challenges

Woman taking part in the Rally of Tunesia

A Challenge is ...

- marrying someone who already has children
- having a career and bringing up a family at the same time
- being a woman in a man's job
- being a man in a woman's job
- overcoming a fear
- going on holiday alone
- starting a new job
- going to a party where you don't know anyone
- organising an event – a wedding, a party
- acting or dancing in front of an audience
- taking up a new sport
- renovating a house or flat
- driving a car through an unknown city
- filling in your tax forms correctly
- reading a book of a 1000 pages

Can you add anything to the list? Compare your ideas in class.

Look at the challenges listed on the poster. Talk to a partner about some of the things

- you have already done and how you dealt with them
- you think you'll do (or do again) in the future
- you think are very easy or difficult to do

→ L & C, p. 75

remember Use **will** to say what you think will happen in the future:

- *I'll probably organise the office party again.*

Will is often used after verbs like *think*, *hope*, *expect*, *know*:

- *I (don't) think I'll look for another job in the next few years.*
- *I expect I'll read Lord of the Rings someday.*

→ Grammar, p. 91

4 A final challenge

Here's a challenge to finish off with.

There are a lot of abbreviations used in e-mails and on the Internet. In groups of three, look at the following common abbreviations and fill in as many of the gaps as possible. After five minutes, compare in class. Who managed the most?

AFAIK	As .... as I ....
FAQ	Frequently asked ....
ASAP	As .... as ....
IMO	In my ....
B4N	Bye ....
TAFN	That's .... now
BTW	By the ....
TTYL	Talk .... you ....
CUL8R	See ....
TYVM	.... you .... much

Tip **Linking words**

In activity 2b you learnt some phrases that are often used in everyday conversation to make what you say more natural and more exciting. Here are some more useful phrases:

- *You won't believe this*
- *(un)fortunately*
- *of course*
- *to my surprise*
- *so*

1 What to say: Structuring a conversation

Dave is talking about a frightening experience. Which of the alternatives is correct? Cross out the incorrect one.

(1) *You won't believe this / You'll never guess what happened* to us on holiday. We were camping in Wales and it was the first evening. (2) *At first / After that* the weather was quite nice but (3) *so / then* it started to get cloudy and (4) *you'll never guess what happened / the next thing we knew* there was a terrible thunderstorm. The tent was really blowing about in the wind. It was quite scary and (5) *to my surprise / of course* we were all absolutely terrified. We managed to hold onto the tent but (6) *suddenly / so* the winds got stronger and the tent just blew away. We didn't know what to do but (7) *fortunately / unfortunately* there was a friendly farmer near the campsite and (8) *in the end / suddenly* we spent the rest of the night there.

2 Pronunciation: Stress – making an account more exciting

When you talk about an experience, you often stress words to make the conversation sound more interesting or exciting. In a sentence you may have a choice of words you can stress: *It was really <u>very</u> good* or *It was <u>really</u> very good* or *It was <u>really very</u> good.*

42 Listen to the dialogue and underline the word or words in each sentence that are stressed the most.

1 A: And then there was this terrible storm.
2 B: Oh, that must have been quite scary.
3 A: Yes, I was absolutely terrified.
4 B: Was there no one there to help you?
5 A: Well, we stopped a car and the driver was very understanding.
6 B: Didn't you feel awfully embarrassed?
7 A: No, we were just so happy to get a lift.

42 Listen again and repeat what you hear.

3 Vocabulary: Please match

Sally is talking to her girlfriend about her next meeting with her boyfriend.
Match the statements with the comments.

1 I have butterflies in my stomach.
2 And I can't eat anything. I feel quite faint.
3 I've put on weight. I feel so self-conscious about it.
4 Last time we met I was on top of the world.
5 I mustn't be so stupid.

☐ a) I know, you felt really great.
☐ b) Yes, you are being rather silly.
☐ c) You always feel nervous before a date.
☐ d) You'd better sit down. You look rather weak.
☐ e) You look good. No need to feel uncomfortable.

p. 79

11 Milestones

1a Memories

Look at the following trends, fashions, etc.

Look at the first four sections of the *Topic vocabulary* and then tell each other what you can remember (or what you have heard) about some of these fashions, films, music trends, etc.? Talk about what you liked and disliked.

I remember (having a skateboard). *Do you remember (E.T.)?* *We used to (wear ...).*
So do / did I. *Oh, I didn't.*

→ Topic vocabulary, p. 76

1950s
Elvis Presley
Rock 'n' roll
Suits and hats for men
Smart dresses for women

1980s
Rap
Breakdance
Skateboards
Film: E.T. the Extra-Terrestrial

1970s
Punks
Disco fever
Film: Star Wars
Platform shoes

1990s
Techno music
Gameboy
Pokemon cards
Film: Titanic

1960s
The Beatles
Hippies
Mini skirts
James Bond films

2000s
Harry Potter mania
Films: Lord of the Rings
Reality TV

Think back to your childhood and adolescence. What was popular then? What sort of music did you listen to? What sort of clothes did you wear? What kind of games did you play? Tell the class.

1b Historical milestones

When did the events below take place? In the late sixties? In the early nineties? Discuss your ideas in small groups and then compare in class.

- First man on the moon
- September 11th
- Wedding of Charles and Diana
- Assassination of J F Kennedy
- Chernobyl
- Balkan crisis
- Introduction of the Euro
- Fall of Berlin wall

In class, brainstorm some more major events that have happened since 1950.

Work in groups of three. Choose some of the events and tell each other about them.

- What do you remember (or know) about them?
- What were you (or your parents) doing at the time?
- Were you (or anyone you know) directly affected by any of the events?

2 The first time

Now choose two of the following "firsts" to talk about. Work in pairs and tell each other how old you were when you did them and give some details.

When was the first time you

- saw the sea / mountains?
- had a boyfriend / girlfriend?
- went on holiday without your family?
- travelled by plane?
- earned some money?
- smoked a cigarette?
- went abroad?

→ L & C p. 76

3 What to say: Interrupting

43 You'll hear Sally telling Simon about the following:

- ☐ a film she's seen
- ☐ an important decision
- ☐ an early memory

Number them in the order you hear them. What does Sally say about each topic?

Now look at the phrases below.

43 Listen again. Which phrase isn't used?

Interrupting
Can I just say something?
Oh, can I ask a question?
Sorry, but ...
Excuse me, but ...

Returning to the topic
Well, anyway, ...
As I was saying, ...

Note: Look at the tip on page 33 to remind you of how to apologise for interrupting.

In groups of three, take it in turns to choose a topic from the list below. The others should interrupt with a question or a comment.

- An early memory
- An experience you didn't enjoy
- An important decision
- A job you didn't like
- A good book you've read
- A good film you've seen
- A play or concert you've been to

remember Use the **present perfect** with *just* to talk about very recent events:

- *I've just finished reading it.*

Use the **present perfect** with time expressions like *ever, never, already* and *yet:*

- *I haven't read it yet.*
- *I've seen it three times already.*

Use the **past simple** with a definite past time:

- *I moved to Germany 18 years ago.*
- *I started the job in 1994.*

→ Grammar, p. 89

4 The ideal age

30% of 26-year-olds still at home

WORKERS TOLD TO RETIRE AT 67

94-YEAR-OLD PASSES DRIVING TEST

What do you think? Is it best to have your first child at 20 or at 40? Write an age next to each question.

What's the best age to

- learn to drive? ☐
- start learning a language? ☐
- leave your parents' house? ☐
- get married for the first time? ☐
- retire? ☐
- have your first child? ☐
- become a grandmother / father? ☐

Compare your answers with one or two other students and say why you chose the age you did. Which of these things have you done? Tell each other how old you were and whether you think it was the ideal age or not.

- *Do you really think so?*
- *Yes, but ...*
- *You're right.*
- *I quite agree with you.*

Do you know anyone who has done something at an unusual age? Tell the class about him / her.

Woman of 52 gives birth

TEEN MARRIAGES ON THE RISE

5 The best years of my life

childhood	adolescence	adulthood	middle age	old age

In class, brainstorm some words and phrases you associate with these different periods in life. Then look at the *Topic vocabulary* and find an adjective to go with each period.

44 You'll hear three senior citizens taking part in a radio programme called "The Best Years of My Life". Listen and note down which periods of life they liked and some of the reasons why. Compare in class.

Talk in small groups.

- What period(s) in your life did you really enjoy and why?
- What do or did you like / dislike about being young, middle-aged or older?

→ Topic vocabulary, p. 76

Tip **Interrupting strangers**

You may want to interrupt a conversation between strangers or people you don't know very well to ask for some information or help. Here are two ways of interrupting politely:

Excuse me for interrupting, but could you tell me where the exit is?
Sorry, may I interrupt for a moment?

1 What to say: Interrupting

Complete the puzzle. Useful tip: Fill in the longest word first. The number of letters in each word is in brackets.

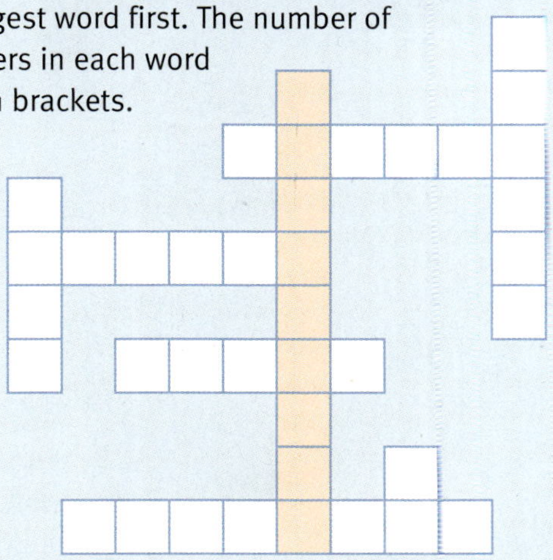

Interrupting

Oh, can I just ask a ~ ? (8)
~ , but can you say that again, please? (5)

Interrupting strangers

~ me for interrupting, but could I open the window, please? (6)
Sorry, may I ~ for a moment? (9)

Apologizing for interrupting

I'm sorry, you ~ saying? (4)
Do ~ on. (2)

Returning to the topic

As I was ~ , we went on holiday to Spain. (6)
Well, ~ , after that we decided to leave. (6)

2 Pronunciation: Stress

Some words in English and German are the same or very similar, but sometimes the word in English is stressed differently. Underline the part of the word where the main stress falls like this: *attractive*

1 balcony	5 problem	9 ideal
2 Chernobyl	6 concert	10 music
3 scandal	7 tolerant	11 programme
4 illegal	8 adolescence	12 culture

Check your answers in the *Key*.

45 Now listen and repeat.

3 Find the right word: A strange couple

Sally was looking out of the window when she suddenly noticed an odd-looking couple walking down the road.
Fill in the gaps with the following words:

baggy, shorter, high-heeled, kind, late, narrow, overweight, ponytail, self-conscious, shirt, skirt, slim

The couple were walking slowly down the (1) .... street. They were in their (2) .... twenties. She looked like a model – tall with long, (3) .... legs. She was wearing a smart, knee-length (4) .... with a pair of red (5) .... shoes. He was quite different. He was a lot (6) .... than she was and a bit (7) .... He had a (8) .... and a beard. He was wearing a pair of (9) .... black trousers with a bright yellow (10) .... He seemed shy and a little (11) .... Certainly not the (12) .... of man you would expect to see her with.

4 Vocabulary: Which words go together?

1 tight-fitting	☐	a) events
2 young	☐	b) sixties
3 disco	☐	c) memories
4 major	☐	d) dress
5 mid	☐	e) fever
6 childhood	☐	f) people

p. 79

12 Learning for life

1 Your skills and abilities

What kind of skill or talent do you wish you had? Would you like to have a good singing voice? be good with your hands? Tell the class.

Now ask questions to find out about other people's skills. If someone answers *yes*, then write his / her name on the line and find out some details (when, how and why they learnt, etc.).

Find someone who can	Name
drive a lorry.	....
install an e-mail programme.	....
do magic tricks.	....
cut someone's hair.	....
make an Advent wreath.	....
make his / her own clothes.	....
do most of the household repairs.	....
do simple first aid.	....
teach someone a skill, a sport, etc.	....

1 Further ideas:
- windsurf
- juggle
- draw
- develop photos
- prune roses

First tell the class one piece of interesting information you heard. Then talk in small groups about any other skills you have or you used to have.

remember Use an **adverb** to say how you do something:
- *I sing badly.*
- *I can add up numbers quite quickly.*

Some adverbs are irregular:
- *I dance well.*

→ Grammar, p. 93

2a Learning experiences

You'll hear Karen and John having a conversation at a class reunion. They use the following expressions:

- low marks
- exam results
- I retrained
- an apprenticeship
- a part-time course

Are there any you don't know? Ask other students what they mean.

46 Now listen and number the topics below (1 to 6) in the order Karen and John talk about them.

- ☐ a skill they found difficult to do
- ☐ a teacher they'll always remember
- ☐ an exam
- ☐ courses at the local community college
- ☐ an unforgettable school memory
- ☐ an enjoyable learning experience

→ L & C, p. 77

2b Class reunion

Look at the *Topic vocabulary* and find some expressions you might need to talk about your learning experiences.

Play the game in groups of three. You should all play on the same board.

Aim of the game: It's your class reunion. You move from table to table talking and answering questions. The player who moves round the room quickest – reaches the "FINISH" first – wins the game.

What you need: Each player needs a small counter (coin, rubber, etc.). You also need one big coin.

Rules: Place your counter on the START. Take it in turns to throw the big coin. Heads: move forward <u>one</u> table; Tails: move forward <u>two</u> tables. Talk about the subject you land on or do what it says. If you land on a free question, the other players should ask you something about your schooling, job training etc.

→ Topic vocabulary, p. 77

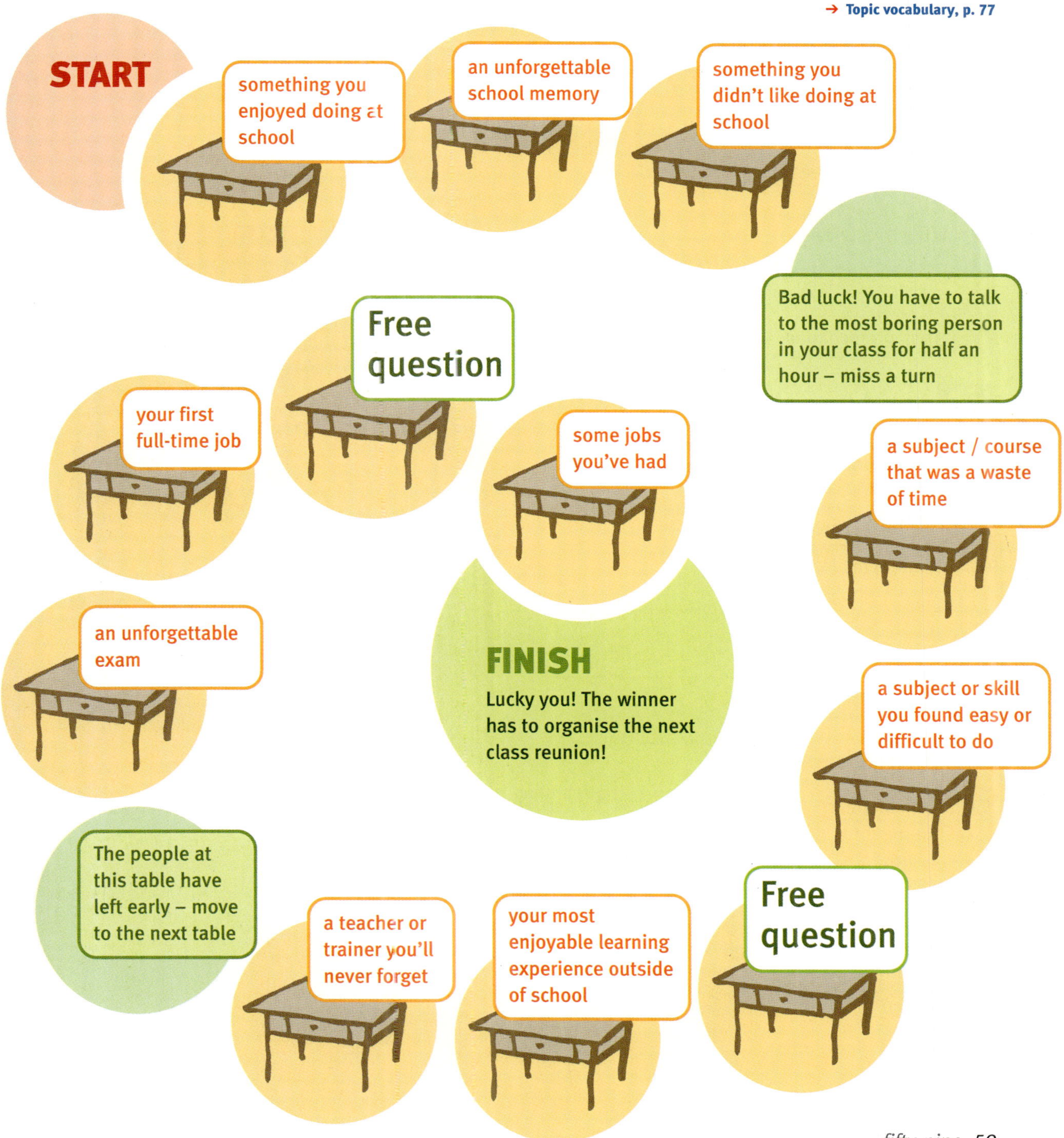

3a What to say: Future plans, giving and reacting to advice

47 You'll hear Leo and Maria talking about some of their future plans. Listen and write down what they still want to do in life.
Now look at the expressions in the box below.

47 Listen again. You'll hear three more expressions. Write them in the box.

Future plans

I'd really like to ...

I'm ....

I'm planning to ...

Giving advice

What ....

You could always ...

Why don't you ...?

Reacting to advice

Well, I think I'd rather ...

Ok, I'll ....

Yes, that's a nice idea.

3b Your future plans

Fill in as many of the following gaps as possible with any skills you'd like to learn or improve or with any courses you'd like to do.

I'd like to .... to help me in my job.

I'd like to .... to improve my English.

I'd like to .... just for fun.

I'd like to .... because I think I'll find it useful.

In small groups, take it in turns to say one thing you'd like to learn in the future and why. Give each other advice on how, where and when they might do this.

4 Talking points

In groups of three, take it in turns to choose one question you'd like to talk about.

1 Does what you learn at school really prepare you for life?
2 What are the differences between school nowadays and when you went to school?
3 How do you think the present school system should be reformed?
4 How can you stay physically and mentally fit in later life?
5 How important is life-long learning?

If you ask me, ...
I think ...,
Yes, but ...,
You're quite right.

Tip **Farewell**

Here are some useful phrases that you can use in the last lesson of your English course:

I've really enjoyed the course. *See you next semester.*

I hope we'll see each other again. *Have a wonderful (summer).*

1 What to say: The end of the course

It's the last lesson of the English course. Daniel and Sarah are having a chat. Rearrange the sentences to find out what Sarah says.

1 been / **It's** / a / it? / great / hasn't / course,

....

....

2 self-conscious / about / first / I / very / **At** / speaking / was / English.

....

....

3 I / all / **But** / we / improved. / think / have

....

....

4 course / planning / to / **I'm** / another / next / do / semester.

....

....

5 too? / in / you / enrol / another / don't / **Why** / course,

....

....

6 get / we / **Maybe** / sometime. / together / can

....

....

7 holiday! / great / a / **Have**

....

Now match each of Daniel's reactions to one of the phrases above. Write the correct sentence number in the box

☐ a) Yes, OK. I'll do that.
☐ b) Oh, so was I.
☐ c) Yes, you're right. We all speak really well now.
☐ d) Really? Another course? That's a good idea.
☐ e) Yes, it certainly has. I've really enjoyed it.
☐ f) You, too.
☐ g) Good idea. Give me a ring.

2 Pronunciation: The sound [ɒ]

The letter "o" is pronounced [ɒ] in words like *concert* when the syllable is stressed and [ə] in words like *lesson* when the "o" is not stressed.

Put a circle round the letter "o" in the following words which have the sound [ɒ]. Remember: If the syllable is not stressed it will be a [ə] sound!

1 economics
2 geography
3 biology
4 conversation
5 photography
6 community
7 college
8 computing
9 pronunciation

Check your answers in the *Key*.

48 Then listen to the words.

3 Vocabulary: All about Carol

At the class reunion Carol told Karen something about her life. Complete the sentences with the correct verb in the past tense: *do, start, work, get, stay, retrain, give up, go, leave*

[1] I (a) .... school at 16 and (b) .... a hairdressing course.

☐ But when I (c) .... pregnant, I (d) .... my training.

☐ I soon got bored alone at home, so I (e) .... back to college and (f) ....

☐ During the course I (g) .... as a trainee at a local hairdresser's.

☐ After retraining I (h) .... my own business and now I have my own hair studio.

☐ I (i) .... at home until my daughter went to school.

Number the sentences above (1-6) in the order you think the events probably took place.

p. 79

Extra 2

Eastern Canada

1 What do you know?

In the eastern part of Canada there are six provinces – Ontario, Quebec, New Brunswick, Nova Scotia, Prince Edward Island and Newfoundland & Labrador.

Talk in class. Do you know anything about these provinces? Look at the photos on these two pages. Do they remind you of anything you know or have read about? What do you know about the other parts of Canada?

2 A TV programme

49 You'll hear three people discussing a TV programme on eastern Canada. They mention the things shown in the photos. Listen and note down what they say about these topics. Compare in class.

What do you now know about eastern Canada that you didn't know before? What did you find particularly interesting? Tell the class.

3 Quiz

Tick (✔) the correct answer.

1. **How many inhabitants live in the six provinces of eastern Canada?**
   - O 12.5 million O 22 million O 32 million
2. **How long does it take to fly from St John's, Newfoundland to Toronto?**
   - O 1 hour O 3 hours O 5 hours
3. **The capital of Canada is**
   - O Toronto O Ottawa O Montreal
4. **Over a quarter of the people of which province were born outside of Canada?**
   - O Nova Scotia O Quebec O Ontario
5. **After the British and the French, which is the largest minority group?**
   - O the Germans O the Italians O the Chinese
6. **In southern Quebec temperatures drop below –20°c**
   - O about once every five years
   - O every winter O in the spring
7. **The Inuit don't like being called "Eskimo" which means**
   - O seal hunter O igloo builder
   - O eater of raw meat
8. **Which First Nation tribe lives in eastern Canada?**
   - O Sioux O Iroquois O Cheyenne
9. **How many official languages are there in Canada?**
   - O one O two O three
10. **In Quebec what percentage of the population count French as their mother tongue?**
    - O 34% O 50% O 85%
11. **In the 1995 referendum in Quebec how many people voted for an independent French-speaking Quebec?**
    - O 35.5% O 49.4% O 50.6%
12. **What is the most popular sport?**
    - O basketball O ice hockey O lacrosse

Mennonites in Ontario

Pow-wow of the Chippewas of Sarnia First Nation, Ontario

Compare your answers with a partner.

- *I think ...*
- *It's definitely ...*
- *Yes, you're right.*
- *Oh I'm afraid I don't agree with you there.*

49 Now listen to the conversation from activity 2 again and check your answers in the *Key*.

p. 80

4 Special feature: Eastern Canada

Imagine you're going to spend a long holiday in the eastern part of Canada. Read about the six provinces and order them according to how much you'd like to visit them. Put a number one next to the province you would most like to visit and so on.

☐ **Ontario**
Capital: Toronto
Population: 12,419,600

Ontario means "glittering water" in the language of the Iroquois and water covers one-sixth of the province. It is home to the Great lakes, Hudson bay, Niagara Falls, the most popular tourist attraction in Canada, and to thousands of lakes and rivers where canoeists and anglers can enjoy the peace and quiet and get the chance to see beavers, moose or even a bear. For the more urban at heart there's Toronto, the financial and commercial centre of Canada, with its fine art museums, luxury stores and cafes, and elegant Ottawa with its mix of historic and modern buildings.

☐ **Quebec**
Capital: Quebec City
Population: 7,529,100

Quebec is an island of French in a sea of North American English and its culture, language, music and way of life are unique. The heart of French Canada is Quebec City, which is Parisian in atmosphere and almost entirely French-speaking. It is also home to the largest winter carnival in the world where people come to watch canoe races in the icy St Lawrence River and to admire the magnificent ice sculptures. Quebec is well known for its maple trees which give up their most famous product – maple syrup – in spring and burst into wonderful colours in autumn and, like Ontario, there are endless forests and numerous lakes where people can enjoy the outdoor life – hiking, canoeing, skiing, snow-shoeing and ice-fishing.

☐ **Prince Edward Island**
Capital: Charlottetown
Population: 141,900

Canada's smallest province is often called Canada's Denmark and with its gently rolling hills, white sandy beaches, sleepy towns and quiet pace of life it is one of Canada's most relaxing provinces. Even the weather is gentler with winter temperatures of around –3 to –11. Most of the population is rural, living in farming communities or in the many small picturesque fishing villages along the coast, where there is a successful lobster industry. Tourists come here to enjoy the cycling and fishing but also to play golf on some of Canada's best golf courses.

Winter carnival in Quebec city

New Brunswick
Capital: Fredericton
Population: 758,000

Canada's largest Atlantic province is bilingual and French-speaking Acadians (17th century French settlers) make up almost 35% of the population. Their culture is alive wherever you go and you can enjoy Acadian music, cuisine and old crafts at their many summer festivals. The coast of New Brunswick is well worth a visit. In the north there are quiet bays and long, sandy beaches and the water temperatures are the warmest to be found north of Florida. In the south, the Bay of Fundy attracts summer visitors who come to see tides of nearly 15 metres, the highest in the world.

Point Prim lighthouse on tip of Digby, Nova Scotia

Nova Scotia
Capital: Halifax
Population: 948,400

Nova Scotia is Latin for New Scotland and although the Scots are now a minority, Scottish culture with its Highland dancing and traditional music of the bagpipes has survived. The province is also famous for its historic towns and villages and for its living-history museums where people in costume re-enact everyday life from the past. The landscape is spectacular and varied. There are dramatic cliffs, picturesque bays, long peaceful beaches, white-wooded houses and lighthouses. Forests cover a large part of the province but in the north there are green pastures and in the west on Cape Breton Island breathtaking mountain scenery and wild moors.

Newfoundland & Labrador
Capital: St John's
Population: 527,300

If you want to get away from it all, this is the place to come. It is the wildest and most isolated of the eastern provinces. It also has some of the most dramatic scenery – steep cliffs, fjords, wild moors and endless forests, home to caribous, moose and black bears. From the coast you can see huge icebergs and whales swimming in the bays. It also has the wildest climate. St John's, the provincial capital, is the foggiest, snowiest, wettest, windiest and cloudiest in the whole of Canada.

Work in groups of three. Compare your order and say why you ordered them as you did. Then tell each other which province you would most / least like to live in if you emigrated to Canada and why. Would your order be the same as if you were spending a holiday there?

5 Over to you

Work in small groups.

1 Think of the country you live in. Tell each other something about other regions that you have been to or know something about.

Indian summer

2 If you wanted to make a programme to show life in your country for Canadian TV what aspects would you include? Decide on a list of things in your groups and then compare in class.

Why don't we ...?
What about ...?
We could ...?
I think we should ...

Everyday activities

have
- breakfast / dinner
- a cup of coffee

do
- the gardening
- the housework
- the washing-up / the ironing

go
- to bed / to work / to church
- (to work) by car
- shopping

take
- the dog for a walk
- your son to football training
- the car to the garage

get
- (a lot of) e-mails / phone calls
- to work / home (early/late)

drive to (work, the shops, etc.)
look after the children / your parents
mow the lawn / cut the grass
feed the dog / baby

! **take:** I take the children to school = Ich bringe die Kinder zur Schule.

Language & culture

Talking to strangers

In many English-speaking countries strangers get into conversation with each other quite easily. It is also a well-known fact that the British talk about the weather, but this is sometimes just an excuse to start a conversation with strangers. Small talk is an important part of everyday life.

People particularly enjoy these little exchanges when they are on holiday or sightseeing and a *Lovely day isn't it?* may just be the beginning of a very pleasant encounter.

If you accidentally bump into someone in the street or open the door for someone with a heavy bag, you will usually exchange a few friendly words or even make a little joke: *Thank you, that's kind of you. I came in to buy some sugar and I seem to have bought half the shop. My husband will have a fit when he sees all these bags!*

When?

in
- the early mornings
- the late afternoons
- the evenings

on
- Tuesdays
- weekdays
- Saturday mornings

at
- about 11 o'clock
- weekends
- night

every
- now and again
- night
- few days/weeks

Where?

at
- home
- work
- school
- the office

next to

! **near:** The church is near our flat.

! **nearby:** The church is nearby.

How do you feel?

fine	not so bad	not very well
great		terrible / awful
very well		rather ill

Exceptional events

get
- married
- divorced
- a new job / promotion

have
- a baby
- an accident
- a bad illness

pass
- an exam
- your driving test

move house leave home retire

Other useful phrases

! **spend time doing:** I spend (all day / a lot of time) phoning clients.

! **have to (past tense):** I had to get up an hour earlier.
I didn't have to drive to work anymore.

Relatives

father-in-law	mother-in-law
brother-in-law	sister-in-law
nephew	niece
grandson	granddaughter

! brothers and sisters: Geschwister

Other people

acquaintance
close friend
next-door neighbour
flatmate
ex-wife / husband
partner
boss
old-age pensioner
senior citizen

! (UK) flatmate
(US) roommate

Where did you meet?

on → a train / a boat / a plane

at → school / work / a party / a friend's house

! at a friend's house: bei einer Freund(in)

When did you meet?

(10) years ago
(quite) recently
in 19../20..
when I was (30)

Useful phrases

I get on really well with ...
I keep in touch with ...
I've lost touch with ...
We see each other (quite often).
We don't see each other very often.
I prefer my own company.
I do quite a lot with ...

Describing people

He / She is
- a loner.
- an individualist.
- a bit eccentric.

He / She has (got)
- a lot of charisma.
- a positive / negative approach to life.

He / She has
- achieved his / her goal in life.
- set an example to others.
- overcome his / her disability.

Language & culture

Entertaining at home

Entertaining at home is very popular in the USA. Americans often invite friends and family over for dinner and in good weather for a barbecue or picnic. Potluck dinners or lunches are also fairly common, where everyone brings along a dish to share with the other guests. Sometimes the host will provide the drinks and ask guests to bring the side dishes and desserts.

Certain important family events are often celebrated with a party. Two American customs are the bridal shower just before a wedding and the baby shower a few weeks before the baby is born. These are essentially gift-giving

events, where everyone will bring along a present for the future bride or mother. A special cake is usually made for the occasion and party games are often played.

Topic vocabulary Unit 3 – Getting around

Ways of travelling

go by bike	cycle, ride a bike
go by bus	take the bus
go by plane	fly
go by car	drive
go on foot	walk

! If you drive a vehicle, you are in control of it.
Compare:
I drive to work.
He drives me to work.

Language & culture

The school run

The school day in the UK usually starts at 9 o'clock and ends between 3.30 and 4pm. Although children go to school later than in most European countries, it does not mean that there is less traffic chaos in the rush hours. This is because of the so-called "school run", when thousands of parents take their children to school in their cars every day although most journeys are less than two miles long. In fact, twice as many parents drive their children to school than they did 20 years ago. For example in Camden in London, there are 29 schools in a one-mile area and around 3,000 cars come every morning and afternoon to drop off and pick up the children. One fifth of the cars on the roads in the rush hours are driven by parents on the school run. The government are asking parents to stop driving their children to school as this causes congestion. They would like children to walk or go by bike if they live close enough to the school.

The British want more US-style school buses.

Useful phrases

The journey takes (two hours).
(The bus) runs (every 20 minutes).
(She) gives me a lift.

Travelling: Useful nouns

road → traffic jam, traffic lights, speed limit, roadworks, cycle path, fine, parking ticket

rail → train connection, platform, fare, intercity supplement

air → connecting flight, landing, take off, terminal

sea → crossing, seasick, cabin

! speed limit: There's a 30 kilometer per hour speed limit.

! roadworks: There are some roadworks in the main street. = Es gibt eine Baustelle in der Hauptstraße.

Adjectives

fast	slow
on time	late
cheap	expensive
safe	dangerous
crowded	empty
stressful	stress-free
reliable	unreliable
environment-friendly	

Types of holiday

go on a/an → package tour / coach tour / cruise / safari / walking holiday / sightseeing holiday / skiing holiday / camping holiday / working holiday / ecological holiday / sailing holiday / wellness holiday / activity holiday

- go on a/an package tour
- go on a/an coach tour
- go on a/an cruise
- go on a/an safari
- go on a/an walking / sightseeing / skiing / camping / working / ecological / sailing / wellness / activity holiday

! Compare:
We went on a walking holiday.
We went walking, skiing, etc.

Places to stay

stay in (a) → luxury hotel / B&B (bed & breakfast) / self-catering accommodation / holiday flat / chalet / villa / cottage / youth hostel

stay on a campsite

!

🇬🇧	holiday flat	campsite
🇺🇸	condo	campground

Adjectives: Describing your holiday

marvellous / amazing / exhausting / awful	holiday
spectacular / breathtaking	scenery
magnificent / impressive	buildings
noisy / quiet / filthy	hotel
unspoilt / picturesque / charming	village
friendly / hospitable	people

Things to do

go walking, fishing, swimming, diving, horse-riding, etc.
go on an excursion, a day trip
go to the seaside, coast, beach
lie on the beach
get a suntan
take photos

Other customs: Useful phrases

respect their culture
adapt to their lifestyle

Language & culture

Australians abroad

About fifty percent of Australians who travel abroad visit English-speaking countries. In 2003 Britain came top of the list with over 720,000 visitors. This is not surprising as over two-thirds of Australia's 19 million people trace their origins to the British Isles. New Zealand came a close second and Australians account for 33% of New Zealand's total number of overseas visitors. Over 500,000 travelled to the United States and Canada. But many Australians visit countries with which Australia does most of its trade, and they are spoilt for choice when it comes to exotic holiday destinations. To the north and east of their continent, the Philippines, Malaysia, Indonesia, China, Japan and countless Pacific islands are places where Australians can enjoy both relaxing and interesting holidays.

Topic vocabulary Unit 5 – Looking after yourself

General

live a healthy life
be health-conscious
be in good / poor health

Exercise and fitness

fit / unfit
be in good / bad shape
be short of breath

! **exercise** = Übung
I do (keep fit / stretching) exercises.

! **exercise** = Bewegung, sich bewegen
I don't do / take / get enough exercise.
I exercise regularly.

Food and diet

health food
junk food
convenience food
be overweight
put on weight
lose weight
be / go on a diet
low-fat diet
My cholesterol is very high / low.

! **overweight:** If you want to be polite, do not say that someone is *fat. (Rather) overweight* is a more polite way of saying the same thing.

Stress

be under stress / pressure
suffer from stress

I feel
- stressed.
- stressed out. *(informal)*
- worried.
- anxious.
- irritated.
- frustrated.
- annoyed.
- impatient.

It really annoys / upsets me.
It doesn't bother me.

! **get + adjective** = werden
I get anxious, irritated, annoyed, etc.

Language & culture

Obesity

The percentage of people who are overweight is now higher than ever before and more and more people are now classed as obese – about 15 kilos or more over the healthy norm. The USA has the highest number of obese people in the world: nearly one-third of the adult population and 15% of adolescents are obese. In Europe, Great Britain is the fattest nation and about 20% of the population is obese, which is three times higher than in 1980.

The fear that fat children will grow into even fatter adults has led to a certain number of initiatives in both the USA and Great Britain. In some areas, schools are no longer allowed to sell sweets and fizzy drinks and are introducing healthy snacks instead. There are also after school fitness clubs for the obese and even summer camps for overweight children.

Free time activities

play →
- table tennis, football, skittles
- cards, board games
- the piano, the trumpet
- in a (local) band, for a club

go →
- jogging, horse-riding, skiing
- for a jog, a walk, a swim
- to the library, to church
- to museums

do →
- judo, karate, yoga
- sport, aerobics, ballroom dancing
- photography, pottery, handicrafts
- crosswords, puzzles
- DIY, the gardening
- the laundry, the cooking

! play **the** piano, play **the** guitar

! **I often go for a walk** = Ich gehe oft spazieren.
I go walking / hiking = Ich gehe wandern.

Useful phrases

I'm (really) good at
I'm (quite) bad at
I'm interested in
I'm keen on
I'd like to take up
→ + gerund or noun (painting, aikido, etc.)

I used to (collect teddy bears, etc.)

I'm a keen footballer, trumpet player.
I'm a sports, rock-and-roll, gardening, cycling enthusiast.
I'm an amateur painter, photographer.

! **I'm a keen golfer. / I'm a golf enthusiast.**
= Ich bin begeisterter Golfer *or* Ich spiele leidenschaftlich gern.
An amateur painter / gardener
= Hobbymaler(in) / Hobbygärtner(in)

Describing an interest or hobby

relaxing	time-consuming
exciting	popular
enjoyable	worthwhile
active	useful
tiring	

You need a lot of patience / strength / stamina.

Unwinding

(Cooking) is a good way of relaxing
switching off
unwinding

I often take time off to relax
to listen to the radio
to sit on the balcony, etc.

Language & culture

Pubs

In Britain a visit to the pub is the most common leisure time activity outside the home. Pubs are places where you can enjoy a drink and a chat and many people regularly go to their "local" – their favourite pub – which is often near where they live. In recent years the pubs have had to change to compete with TV, clubs and cinemas. The opening hours are now more flexible and most pubs offer snacks or hot meals. In the morning they are open for coffee and children are now allowed in some pubs during the day, especially those which have a beer garden. There are usually two rooms in the pub; the public bar which is used more by men and the more comfortable lounge bar used by both men and women. Games such as darts and billiards are usually played in the public bar and there is often a satellite television where people watch important sports events together. On some evenings there is often a general knowledge quiz, karaoke or live music, which appeal to all age groups. Another activity, popular with young people, is the so-called pub-crawl, which involves going from one pub to another having a drink in each one.

What's it like?

ugly	attractive	beautiful
clean	dirty	polluted
noisy	quiet	
boring	lively	
dangerous	safe	
isolated	easy to reach	
urban	rural	

size → huge / large / medium-sized / small

streets → narrow / wide

Where is it?

in the north of (Germany)
about ... kilometres west of (Vienna)
on the east coast of ...
on a river
on an island
in the mountains
near the border, a wood, the sea

I live in → the country. / the suburbs. / the / an industrial area. / the town centre. / a residential area.

I live on → the outskirts (of the town). / a major road.

Language & culture

When I'm 65

77% of the people in Britain live in towns but many dream of living in the country or by the sea. When they reach retirement age, senior citizens are often able to realise this dream. They are quite prepared to leave an area they have lived in for many years in order to start a new life at 65. They sell their house (nearly 70% of the British own their own homes) and move to a bungalow in a small coastal town, to housing estates for the elderly, or to a retirement village. In many communities, on the south coast of England for example, where the climate is milder, three-quarters of the people are pensioners.

In contrast, in order to enjoy their years of retirement many Canadians simply prefer to leave Canada in the winter to get away from the cold and the snow. Half a million retired Canadians spend the winter in Florida. These so-called "snowbirds" spend three to six months down south, where they can live comfortably in a condominium complex with a swimming pool. As they have no problems with the language or the food the Canadians feel quite at home. They usually head back to their homes in Canada about mid-April to take up their normal lives once again.

Useful phrases

It has a population of (over) ...
What's the population of ...?

I was born in ...
I grew up in ...
I've spent most of my life in ...

What's the weather like?

cloudy	wet
foggy	dry
sunny	humid
windy	changeable

You (don't) get a lot of rain / sun.
The temperature often reaches ... / drops to ...

flood
hurricane
thunderstorm
blizzard
heavy / light rain

Topic vocabulary

Communicating with others

send / get → an e-mail, a letter, a memo, a message, a text message

make / get — a phone call

keep in touch → via e-mail, via text messaging

book a flight online
reserve a seat online
leave a message on the answering machine

Computer / Internet

floppy disc	printer	loudspeaker
screen	mouse	microphone
keyboard	mousepad	scanner

surf the (Inter)net

lose / delete / save → a / the file

make a back up file

Mobile phone

! 🇺🇸 Cell phone

I use a prepaid phone card.
I have a fixed contract.

local / long-distance / urgent → call

Useful gadgets

fridge
freezer
cooker
oven
microwave
electric kettle
coffee machine
dishwasher

electric toothbrush
electric razor
hairdryer
washing machine

tumble dryer
iron
vacuum cleaner

electric drill
lawnmower
DVD player
video recorder
CD player
calculator
photocopier
(telephone) answering machine

Technical breakdown

There was something wrong with the ...
It didn't work.
It wouldn't start.
It made a strange noise.
It had an electrical / a mechanical fault.
It was faulty.

The computer crashed.

repair / mend / fix → a gadget, a machine, etc.

! **I had it mended.** = Ich habe es/sie/ihn reparieren lassen.

Language & culture

SMS Texting

Nearly everyone is only a mobile phone call away! You can contact people 24 hours a day, and you don't even have to interrupt their lives by phoning them, you can simply text a message. Texting is a quick and cheap alternative to the phone call and it saves time, too. In the UK 70% of the population send text messages and over 12 billion messages are sent each year – and the numbers are on the rise. Speed texting – saying as much as you can in as short a way as possible – has become a kind of sport and created a whole new language: CU2niteB4party. Some mobiles have an in-built dictionary that can guess what you are writing. On a day like Valentine's day over a billion messages are texted, but even on an ordinary day over half of the messages sent are to loved ones. So if you think that sending text messages is a "good way to flirt", then you should try one of the bars which have text-flirting evenings – the newest way to find a partner.

Topic vocabulary Unit 9 – Money matters

Money vocabulary

save / spend / waste / invest / inherit / earn / borrow / lend / lose → money

buy / sell → shares

take out a bank loan

! borrow and lend:

I borrowed some money from the bank.
The bank lent me some money.

How to pay

pay →
- cash
- by credit card
- by debit card
- by store (credit) card
- by cheque
- by bank transfer
- by direct debit

Types of shops

department store
corner shop
shopping centre / mall
market
baker's
butcher's
greengrocer's
chemist's
newsagent's
florist's
jeweller's

Useful shopping words

It's →
- cheap.
- expensive.
- reduced (by 20%).
- half price.
- a special offer.
- a bargain.

They're sold out.

! bargain = günstiges Angebot

I'll buy a TV if I can find a bargain at the sales.
It was a real bargain. = Es war super günstig.

Useful phrases

You get good value for money.
The prices are reasonable.
There's a wide choice.
The shop assistants are friendly / helpful.
The customer / delivery service is excellent.
They sell unusual products.
It's good / bad quality.
You can exchange your goods / get your money back.

I order things from →
- the Internet.
- mail order catalogues.

Language & culture

Super malls

Super malls, which are now also found in the UK, are huge shopping centres on the outskirts of the cities. They are "virtual cities" with an incredible choice of shops, cafés, restaurants, clubs and cinemas. Many shoppers will tell you that the mall is much better than the real city centre; here the temperature never changes. There's no more carrying heavy bags up the high street in the pouring rain, no litter and no beggars. Security guards are there to make sure that everything is safe and kept under control. Bluewater, which opened in Kent, England in 1999, is the largest shopping centre in Europe, with seven lakes, natural light, "real" fresh air, a revolving dance floor and 320 stores and restaurants. There are radio-controlled mini boats for children to play with and for bored husbands or boyfriends there's a "male crêche", where they can have a drink and catch up with the sports. Bluewater attracts over 30 million "guests" every year. Metroland in Gateshead in the north-east of England, Trafford Centre, Manchester and Lakeside in Essex are three more popular Super malls, which offer a wonderful day out for the whole family.

Useful adjectives

brave
calm

worried / anxious / nervous → about

afraid / scared / frightened / terrified → of

! I'm: frightened, terrified, scared
It's: frightening, terrifying, scary

Useful phrases

It makes me feel uneasy / nervous.
My heart beats faster.
My legs shake.
I'm short of breath.
I have a dry mouth.
I have butterflies in my stomach.
I start to sweat.
I feel faint.
I faint.

How did you feel?

I felt / was → really / very / quite → nervous / frightened.

I was absolutely terrified.

I felt → fine. / great / wonderful. / on top of the world. / awful.

I felt / was → uncomfortable. / self-conscious. / embarrassed.

Challenges

I tried to ...
I managed to ...
I succeeded in (+ing)
I'd refuse to ...

It's → easy / difficult / (almost) impossible → to

Language & culture

Challenged?

Do you know anyone who is *horizontally*, *visually* or *physically challenged*? Well, if you do, you might simply say the person is fat, blind or handicapped, but if you want to be more *politically correct* (PC), you would certainly use, *overweight*, *visually disabled* and *physically disabled*. Most people find expressions like *horizontally challenged* a little exaggerated, but by using politically correct expressions you avoid offending people and this helps to change attitudes and behaviour. In the U.S.A, *political correctness* has influenced the development of language since the 1970s and people are extremely careful about the expressions they use in public. In the UK, everyday language has been influenced by PC language: *Senior citizen* is more acceptable than old-age pensioner, *flight attendant* has replaced air hostess and *developing countries*, Third World countries.

Snowperson

Age

in the	early mid late	sixties / nineties, etc.

when I was	a teenager young / middle-aged (about) 24

when I was in my	early mid late	teens / thirties, etc.

Language & culture

Fashions come and go – smoking habits

Over a hundred years ago Oscar Wilde, the famous Irish writer, spoke for many when he wrote "A cigarette is the perfect type of a perfect pleasure". How different things would seem to Wilde if he were in Ireland today. Since March 2004 it has become illegal in the whole of the country to smoke in the workplace, which means that bars and restaurants have also become smoke-free zones. Many people fear that the Irish pub, with its tradition of a cigarette and a pint of beer, will become a much less attractive place. But do the Irish really need to worry? In California and New York the ban on smoking in restaurants has not had a negative effect on business. On the contrary, custom has increased. So it looks as if non-smokers, who are after all in the majority, are winning the battle and smokers will now have to go outside whenever they want to light up.

Clothes and fashion

suit, trousers, shirt, belt, tie
dress, skirt, blouse, scarf

smart, long, wide, baggy
casual, short, narrow, tight-fitting
knee-length

platform / high-heeled / low-heeled → shoes / boots

Appearance

long / short / shoulder-length / permed → hair

I had a plait / plaits.
I had a ponytail.

beard
moustache

I wore make-up.

I was slim.
I was attractive.
I was good-looking.

Children's games

play → marbles / hide and seek / tag

ride → a bike / a scooter

skip · roller-skate · inline-skate

Useful adjectives

self-conscious	(in)experienced
shy	self-confident
rebellious	responsible
independent	sensitive
energetic	successful
(in)tolerant	lonely

Skills

I know how to ...
I learnt how to ...
I taught myself to ...

Places of learning

playgroup	grammar school
nursery school	comprehensive school
primary school	single sex school
secondary school	boarding school
college	adult education centre
university	evening classes

! **Note:** It is difficult to find exact equivalents in English for the type of school you attended, the exams you took, etc. You may want to use a general term and not be too specific.

Mittlere Reife, Hauptschulabschluss, Abitur = school-leaving exam

Gymnasium, Realschule, Hauptschule = secondary school

! **community college**
This is the German Volkshochschule, Berufsschule and Abendgymnasium all in one.
It offers courses in aerobics, photography and French conversation but also has courses for people who want to train for jobs or study for public examinations.

School subjects

maths	chemistry	art
science	biology	geography
economics	physics	history

Exams and qualifications

take / pass / fail → an / the exam

I did → my school-leaving exam. / a diploma. / my final exams.

I got good / bad grades.

I'm → a qualified (engineer, dentist). / a trained (nurse, secretary). / a master (chef, carpenter).

Training

I studied (chemistry).

I took a full-time / part-time course in (computing).

I trained as a (bank clerk).
I retrained as a (dental assistant).
I served / did an apprenticeship as a (printer).
I did an in-service training course / some further training.
I'm an experienced (teacher).

! **apprentice / trainee**
In Britain, an apprentice learns a skill or a trade (baker, car mechanic, plumber).
A trainee is used for other jobs (nurse, teacher, secretary, sales manager).

Language & culture

UK education system

About 90% of schoolchildren in the UK attend state schools. The remainder go to private schools (so-called independent schools) or are educated at home (about 1%). Most children in the state education system go to a primary school between the ages of 4 and 5 and then at the age of 11 they move to a comprehensive school, which teaches children of all abilities. At 16 pupils take GCSEs (General certificate of education) in a variety of subjects. All children must stay at school until they are 16. Some pupils then leave school and start work, or go to a college to do a vocational course. But many now choose to stay on at school to study for academic qualifications called A-levels (Advanced level), which are usually taken at the age of 18. Students specialise in two or three subjects from the wide choice available – anything from maths and history to business studies and economics to drama and photography. They usually need to pass 3 A-levels in order to go to university.

Key Selfstudy, Grammar check, Extra

Unit 1

1 1 Yes, it's already six o'clock. I'll let you get back to your family.; Say hello to Frank for me.; Bye. See you next week. 2 Yes, it's been really nice talking to you, too.; Yes, good idea. Give me a ring sometime.; Bye. And don't forget to ring.

2 1 sist(er), 2 c(a)ssette, 3 ev(e)n, 4 (a)fraid, 5 acc(e)nt, 6 pregn(a)nt, 7 less(o)n, 8 t(o)night, 9 breakf(a)st

3 do: the gardening, the housework, a language course; get: married, divorced, home; have: a chat, a baby, problems; 1 got home, 2 do a language course, 3 had a baby, 4 do the housework, 5 getting married / going to get married, 6 have a chat

Unit 2

1 1a) Sorry, I couldn't quite follow that. 1b) I'm afraid I didn't quite understand what you said. 2a) Could you say that again, please? 2b) Sorry, can / could you repeat that, please? 3a) Sorry, that was a bit too fast. 3b) Can / Could you speak more slowly, please? 4a) Sorry, I'll start again. 4b) What I mean is ... 5a) Oh, I see. 5b) I've got it now.

2 1 same, 2 different, 3 same, 4 different, 5 different, 6 different, 7 same, 8 different, 9 different, 10 different

Voiced sounds: 1 (j)ob, (G)erman, 2 (j)azz, 3 mana(g)er, emer(g)ency, 4 (th)is, 5 (th)at, 8 clo(s)ed, 9 o(f), 10 li(v)e

3 1 acquaintance, 2 grandson, 3 nephew, 4 husband, 5 colleague, 6 partner, 7 sister-in-law

4 1 c, 2 e, 3 d, 4 b, 5 a

Unit 3

1 1 So do I. Especially in good weather. 2 Neither can I. Everyone drives too fast. 3 Oh, I haven't. But I must buy one next week. 4 So did I. It was very cheap. 5 Oh, I'm not. My husband's giving me a lift. 6 Neither would I. I don't like heights.

2 1 h, 2 d, 3 f, 4 g, 5 i, 6 c, 7 a, 8 b, 9 e

3 1 bicycle, 2 appropriate, 3 automatic, 4 balloon, 5 travelling, 6 connection, 7 roadworks, 8 apparently

A: I'm sometimes airsick.	B: So am I.
A: She isn't afraid of flying.	B: Neither is he.
A: They wouldn't do it.	B: But we would.
A: I often cycle in the city centre.	B: Oh, we don't.

4 1 missing, 2 to get, 3 to drive, 4 travelling, 5 taking, 6 using, 7 to do, 8 taking

Unit 4

1 a) Rather you than me. It's a long flight. b) Congratulations! Tell me all about her. c) Lucky you. I'd love to do that. d) Oh no! What an awful start to your holiday! e) All week? How awful! f) Really? I didn't know it was so primitive. g) Oh, I'm sorry to hear that. Perhaps you can go later in the year. h) Sounds lovely! Were there palm trees, too?

2 1 great, 2 good, 3 dream, 4 country, 5 weather, 6 on

3 1 wonderful, 2 impressive, 3 charming, 4 breathtaking, 5 terrified, 6 filthy, 7 dreadful, 8 friendly, 9 exhausting

4 1 They've gone to Paris. 2 We've been abroad many times. 3 Have you ever been to Spain? 4 I think he's gone on holiday. 5 She's been to Minorca.

Unit 5

1 1 haven't we? 2 don't we? 3 are there? 4 isn't it? 5 didn't she? 6 wasn't it? 7 were they? 8 do you?;
2 a, 4 b, 7 c

2a 2 and 4 are real questions.

2b 1 voucher, variety, vegetables,
2 chocolate, Chinese, chewing gum,
3 cholesterol, Christmas, alcoholic,
4 comprehensive, conscious, convenience,
5 recipe, subscription, insomnia,
6 homeopathic, healthy, aromatherapy

3 1 bring up, 2 suffers from, 3 eats, 4 to live, 5 to exercise, 6 to go on, 7 to lose, 8 to give up, 9 is

Unit 6

1 1 you were saying? 2 please continue. 3 Oh sorry. Carry on. 4 Sorry. Do go on.

2 a 2, b 1, c 2;
1 Let's go for a walk. 2 How about a glass of wine? 3 It's as good as mine. 4 He goes to church regularly. 5 When he was a young man he played in a band. 6 Jogging can be more tiring than swimming.

3 1 at, on, for, 2 on, off, 3 about, off, 4 of, 5 at, at, 6 at, 7 up, 8 in

Unit 7

1 Incorrect are: 1 c, 2 b, 3 c, 4 c, 5 b, 6 a.

2 1 very, 2 really, 3 too, 4 quite, 5 rather, 6 so

3 1 Well, personally, I think the people are very nice. 2 And the shops are just great. 3 I think the local school is quite good, too. 4 If you ask me, the kids are much happier here.;
1 d, 2 c, 3 b, 4 a
4 1 f, 2 e, 3 g, 4 h, 5 b, 6 i, 7 a, 8 d, 9 c

Unit 8

1 1 use for, 2 sort of, 3 used for, 4 that, 5 made of, 6 flat, square. Electric drill and floppy disc.
2 1 That wasn't such a useful device after all.
2 It's used for sending messages.
3 He didn't use to use the phone so much.
4 It's something he doesn't often use.
5 This old cell phone of yours isn't much use.
3 1 down, 2 wrong, 3 strange/funny noises, 4 fault
4 Incorrect are: 1 town, 2 became, 3 ordered, 4 left, 5 look for

Unit 9

1 2, 4, 1, 6, 7, 3, 5

2 1
2
3
4
5
6

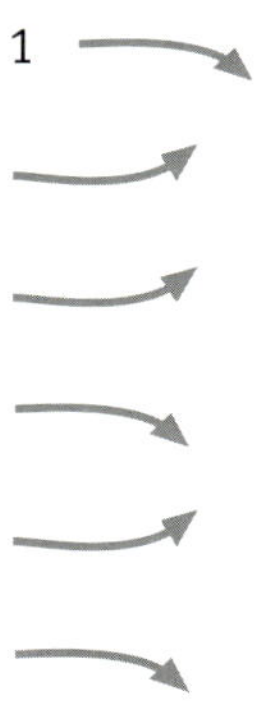

3 1 trip, fun 2 service, assistants, 3 prices, value 4 choice, quality 5 offers, bargains

Unit 10

1 Correct are: 1 You'll never guess what happened, 2 At first, 3 then, 4 the next thing we knew, 5 of course, 6 suddenly, 7 fortunately, 8 in the end
2 1 And then there was this terrible storm.
2 Oh, that must have been quite scary.
3 Yes, I was absolutely terrified.
4 Was there no one there to help you?
5 Well, we stopped a car and the driver was very understanding.
6 Didn't you feel awfully embarrassed?
7 No, we were just so happy to get a lift.
3 1c, 2d, 3e, 4a, 5b

Unit 11

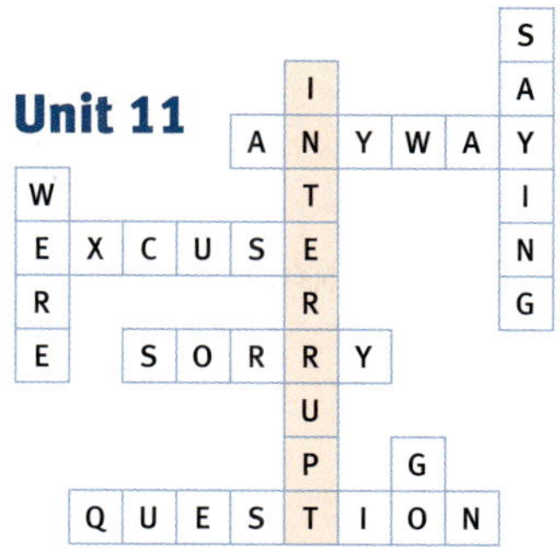

2 1 balcony, 2 Chernobyl, 3 scandal, 4 illegal, 5 problem, 6 concert, 7 tolerant, 8 adolescence, 9 ideal, 10 music, 11 programme, 12 culture
3 1 narrow, 2 late, 3 slim, 4 skirt, 5 high-heeled, 6 shorter, 7 overweight, 8 ponytail, 9 baggy, 10 shirt, 11 self-conscious, 12 kind
4 1 d, 2 f, 3 e, 4 a, 5 b, 6 c

Unit 12

1 1 It's been a great course, hasn't it? 2 At first I was very self-conscious about speaking English. 3 But I think we have all improved. 4 I'm planning to do another course next semester. 5 Why don't you enrol in another course, too? 6 Maybe we can get together sometime. 7 Have a great holiday!;
1 e, 2 b, 3 c, 4 d, 5 a, 6 g, 7 f
2 1 econ(o)mics, 2 ge(o)graphy, 3 bi(o)logy, 4 c(o)nversation, 5 phot(o)graphy, 7 c(o)llege
3 a) left, b) did, c) got, d) gave up, e) went, f) retrained, g) worked, h) started, i) stayed
1, 3, 5, 2, 6, 4

Grammar Check

1a do, be, have
1b 1 on Mondays, 2 today, 3 the last two years, 4 never, 5 in 2001, 6 when
2a 1b, 2d, 3c, 4a
2b am (I'm) having, 2 isn't doing, 3 gets, 4 refuses, 5 watches, 6 doesn't listen, 7 is ('s) taking
3a 1b, 2e, 3d, 4a, 5c
3b Correct are: 1 was raining, 2 went, 3 was driving, 4 noticed, 5 got out, 6 phoned
4a 1b, 2d, 3a, 4c
4b 1 have ('ve) been looking, 2 have ('ve) been driving, 3 have ('ve) looked, 4 have ('ve) never seen, 5 have ('ve)decided
4c 1 since he came in (•), for over six hours (⟿), since 9 o'clock, (•) 2 for a long time (⟿), since 1988 (•), for over 30 years (⟿)
5a are you and Steve going to do, are('re) going to invite, am ('m) not going to cook, is ('s) going to order, are ('re) going to enjoy

6a 1 will work, 2 will have to, 3 will suffer from, 4 will live, 5 will improve
6b 1 d, 2 a, 3 b, 4 c
7a a) Typ 2, b) Typ 1
7b 1 will, 2 would, 3 will, 4 would
8a 1 a lot of, 2 much, 3 a lot of / much, 4 many, 5 much, 6 many, 7 a lot of / much
9a 1 the keenest / cheaper, 1a bigger / fittest, 2 cleverer / healthiest, 2a more famous / most useful, 3 most dangerous / more interesting
9b 1 most common, 2 easier / than, 3 more flexible, 4 more comfortable, 5 popular / as, 6 best
10a Correct are: 1 beautifully / well, 2 perfectly / fluently, 3 hard / quickly, 4 badly / fast, 5 warmly, enthusiastically
11a 1 didn't use to do, 2 used to wash, 3 did you use to do
12a 1 driving, 2 to drive, 3 to drive, 4 driving

Extra 1

1 Quiz **1** 2.9 million (United Kingdom has a population of 59 million). **2** Cardiff (Cardiff was chosen as the national capital in 1955). **3** Snowdon, North Wales (1,085 m) (Sugar Loaf, South Wales (596 m), Ben Nevis, Scotland (1,343 m)). **4** 1997. The Welsh voted for an independent assembly for Wales in 1997. (In 1999 The National Assembly of Wales was formed). **5** English (Erse is a Gaelic language spoken in Ireland). **6** 20% (Today over 500,000 people speak Welsh. At the start of the 20th century it was 900,000). **7** 1998 (Welsh lessons compulsory up to age of 16). **8** Patagonia (In May 1865, led by Michael Jones, 163 Welsh men, women and children left for Patagonia to establish a Welsh-speaking community. It has survived to the present day and Patagonia also has some bilingual schools). **9** daffodil (Thistle is the emblem of Scotland. The rose is thought of as a typically English flower). **10** dragon (When Henry VII became King of England in 1485, he decided that the Red Dragon should be known as the official flag of Wales). **11** rugby (It is said that rugby football was first played in the 1890s at Rugby school, a famous public school). **12** Tom Jones (He was born in Pontypridd, Wales in 1940. His full name is Thomas Jones Woodward. He chose Tom Jones because he wanted to be associated with Wales). **13** 1284 (In 1536 the Act of Union was passed under Henry VIII, completing the political and legal union with Wales). **14** 1969, at the age of 21 (Prince Charles was born in 1948. He married Lady Diana Spencer in 1981).

2 A week in Wales **1 Opens conversation:** Well, hi there. I haven't seen you for ages. Nice to see you again after such a long time. How are things? **2 Keeps the conversation going:** **a Reacting and encouraging:** Sounds great, Oh, no, those Welsh names! Yeah? Oh, is it? Really, Is that right? Sounds lovely. **b Repeats words:** Wales!, Gwyneth Jones? Oh, the Eisteddfod! **c Asks questions:** e.g. Are you going on vacation? Where to? To where? That's a Welsh name, isn't it? You aren't related to the great Welsh poet, are you? So what about Tom Jones? Is he Welsh? Gwyneth Jones, who's she? Anyway, what are you doing in Thl....? Isn't that where all the poets and singers meet? **3 Closes conversation:** Hey, look at the time. I'm afraid I must rush back to the office. Duty calls. Say "hi" to Sandra for me. We must all get together soon.

Extra 2

3 Quiz **1** 22 million (12.5 million live in Ontario and 32 million in the whole of Canada). **2** 3 hours (It takes 5 hours to fly from St John's to London and 9 hours from St John's to Vancouver which is on the west coast of Canada). **3** Ottawa (Toronto is the largest city in Canada (pop. 4.5 million) and Montreal is the second largest (pop. 3.3 million)) **4** Ontario (26.8% of the people in Ontario are foreign born, 9.9% of the population of Quebec and 4.6% of the people in Nova Scotia). **5** the Germans (Many German immigrants have settled in the area around Kitchener, Ontario. Kitchener was originally called Berlin but was renamed in World War I). **6** every winter (The average maximum daytime temperature in January is about -8°c in southern Quebec and southern Ontario). **7** eater of raw meat (Inuit means the people). **8** Iroquois (Sioux and Cheyenne live in the USA). **9** two (English and French). **10** 85% (35% of the people in New Brunswick are French-speaking). **11** 49.4%. **12** ice hockey (But lacrosse is the official national game).

Ein Ziel von *English Network Basic Conversation* ist es, besonders Ihr Hörverstehen zu verbessern. Vielleicht möchten Sie deshalb nach dem Unterricht nochmals einige Dialoge anhören. Hier haben wir einige der umfangreicheren Texte für Sie zum Nachlesen abgedruckt, falls Sie noch mehr Details verstehen möchten.

Unit 2, Activity 2a: People in our Lives: A radio interview

Mike: I'd like to introduce our special guest today, Maria Brian, who's taken time off her busy tour to be with us here today. Hi, Maria.

Maria: Hello, Mike. It's good to be here.

Mike: We have a lot of listeners who want to get to know you as a private person, not Maria the star, but Maria as her family and friends know her.

Maria: That's OK with me.

Mike: OK, the first question, please. And it's from Jean.

Jean: Maria, I'd like to know who you spend a lot of time with.

Maria: Ah, at the moment with my bank manager. No, that's not true. Um ... well ... I spend a lot of time with the band, of course, especially before a big concert – we work a lot on the melodies together. And ... um, I still spend a lot of time with my son, Simon. We cook and watch a lot of TV together. You know, I'm a single mother and so when I'm home I do quite a lot with him. Mind you, he's 17 now and sometimes he prefers to be with his friends. It's no longer cool to be seen with his mum.

Mike: Yeah, yeah.

Maria: Anyway, when he's not there and I'm not working I spend a lot of time on my own. I find I really enjoy it. I just love curling up on the sofa with a good book or listening to some good jazz. Yeah, that about answers that one.

Mike: OK, thanks Jean, Maria. Let's have our next caller. Tim, are you there?

Tim: Yeah, hi, Maria.

Maria: Hello, Tim.

Tim: My question is – Who do you rely on in an emergency?

Maria: You mean, an emergency like I've almost cut my finger off with a bread knife and I need help quickly – like really quickly.

Tim: Yeah, yeah.

Maria: Well, I have these great neighbours – they're over seventy and they haven't got any children. I once woke them up in the middle of the night because I'd cut my leg on a broken bottle and they took me to the hospital.

Mike: They sound wonderful.

Maria: They're a great help. And I can always phone my sister-in-law, Susie, she's my ex's elder sister. I get on really well with her and ... um ... anyway, if I'm ill or anything, she'll come over and help. She'll do the shopping and make sure my son still washes behind his ears and things. Yeah. Does that answer your question, Tim?

Tim: Yeah, great. Thanks, Maria.

Mike: I think we have time for one or two more questions. Wendy would like to ask a question.

Wendy: OK, Maria, which people do you keep in touch with? You know, who do you often write to or call?

Maria: My mum. We phone regularly. Actually, I'm not much of a letter writer. I have a secretary who looks after all my work correspondence. And I'm really happy about that. Um ... but I keep in touch with some of my old schoolfriends. One lives in Japan so we don't see each other very often but we send each other a mail sometimes and Christmas cards, photos of the kids and things like that.

Wendy: Thanks, Maria.

Maria: It's been nice talking to you, Wendy.

Mike: And our final caller is Charlotte. Charlotte, your question, please?

Charlotte: Yeah, Maria, um ... ah ... who would you lend your car to?

Maria: My car? That's a difficult one to answer. I've got two cars now – a great sports car that I never lend to anyone. There's no one I'd trust with my Porsche. Then I've got a fairly old Volvo. Since my son passed his driving test he borrows it all the time. In fact, I usually have to ask him if I can use it.

Mike: OK. Thanks a lot, Charlotte. Stay tuned. We'll be talking to Maria some more after these commercials.

Unit 3, Activity 4: A Nightmare Journey

Lynne: Oh, hello, Brian.

Brian: Hi, Lynne. How are things?

Lynne: Not too good this morning.

Brian: I'm sorry to hear that. What's wrong?

Lynne: Why don't you come in and I'll tell you all about it.

Lynne: Sit down.

Brian: Thanks. So did something happen down in London?

Lynne: London was fine. It was the journey home. It was a nightmare. I didn't get home until 8 o'clock this morning.

Brian: 8 o'clock? Why? What happened?

Lynne: Do you want the whole story?

Brian: Yeah, yeah, tell me all about it.

Lynne: Well, I caught the ten o'clock train from London, which of course left about 20 minutes late. Apparently they couldn't find a driver.

Brian: Oh no!

Lynne: Anyway, the train started and everything was OK. But then about an hour later I was just falling asleep when suddenly the train stopped – in the middle of nowhere. No explanations, of course! Everyone was really fed up.

Brian: So what was the problem?

Lynne: The problem? Well, after we'd sat there for ages they apologised for the delay. There was a signals failure.

Brian: Yeah. And what happened then?

Lynne: Well, they said the train would move as soon as possible and that they were very sorry, etc. etc. But do you know how long we sat there? Four hours. It was four hours before we moved.

Brian: Oh, that's terrible!

Lynne: You can imagine the atmosphere. People were not happy. Anyway, four hours later we set off again. We were still only a bit north of Bedford and suddenly they said the train would terminate at Kettering because the line was closed for repairs.

Brian: Oh, so what did you do?

Lynne: I was just too tired to react by this time but there was one guy in our compartment – we had to stop him attacking the ticket collector!

Brian: Yeah, I can just imagine that.

Lynne: Well, they promised there'd be a luxury coach to take us to Nottingham, but when we arrived at Kettering – at 4 o'clock in the morning! – there was this old, dirty double-decker bus waiting by the platform. I mean, I was so exhausted, I didn't mind but some of the others ... well, I won't tell you what they said, especially when taxis arrived to take the train crew home. It was just too much. And it was raining.

Brian: Oh no! How awful!

Lynne: I haven't finished yet. We had to wait then about twenty minutes on this horrible bus for some other passengers. Their trains had been delayed, too.

Brian: Oh ... So when did you get home?

Lynne: We arrived in Nottingham just after 7. What a journey! It took nine hours instead of three.

Brian: That's unbelievable. Do you know that you can fly from London to Bombay in nine hours?

Unit 4, Activity 4: Different countries, different customs

Rob: Yes, it was a great holiday. The people are very hospitable and make you very welcome. We were even invited to dinner.

Friend: Yeah. Great!

Rob: Yes, ... well ... it was an interesting experience. We arrived at about 9 o'clock.

Friend: 9 o'clock? 9 o'clock in the evening? That's a bit late, isn't it?

Rob: Yeah, they often eat their main meal quite late ... um ... at about 10. It's cooler then. And anyway, we had to wait for the other guests to arrive. Their idea of time is completely different from ours. So if they invite you for nine o'clock, it's quite alright if you turn up at 10.

Friend: Really? I didn't know that. So did you like the food?

Rob: Ah ... that was my big mistake. I really liked the food but I ate mine too quickly and our host then just continued filling up my plate and you know, you're not allowed to say no. You just have to eat it. I was completely full.

Friend: Oh, right. So... um ... what else did you do?

Rob: Well ... mm ... we did quite a lot of sightseeing.

Friend: In that heat?

Rob: Yeah, it was boiling hot. And you can't go round in shorts and sleeveless T-shirts, although some tourists do that. You really have to be careful what you wear. My wife was always careful to cover her shoulders and wear long skirts.

Friend: Yeah, yeah.

Rob: Mm ... what I really loved were the bazaars.

Friend: Oh yeah, did you bring home lots of souvenirs?

Rob: Yes, we bought quite a lot – quite a lot of jewellery but I'm sure we paid far too much for it. You know, they love haggling over prices. I think it's their favourite pastime so if you want to buy something, you're expected to do it, too.

Friend: And what were the pyramids like?

Rob: Oh, they were just fantastic.

Sarah: The food was delicious. There were just hundreds of types of soups, noodles, rice dishes, fruits and vegetables – there was always something good to eat. But I had problems using chopsticks and I really missed my toast for breakfast.

Friend: So what did you have?

Sarah: Well, you know, they often have a rice dish for breakfast, too.

Friend: Mm, it's healthier than toast.

Sarah: Yeah, I guess you're right. But I still missed it and I missed having a good cup of coffee, too. They drank so much tea. They have these wonderful teahouses where people just go to chat or play cards or majong.

Friend: It's better than watching TV, huh?

Sarah: Yeah, people often seemed to do things together. In the early mornings you often saw groups of people doing tai chi. And a lot of older people did it, too. In fact, I really wanted to join in.

Friend: Yeah, so you liked their way of life, then.

Sarah: Well, it was definitely different and the people were fascinating. Oh, we got to know a family there and that was really interesting. Just having a conversation with them is amazing. They ... um ... they have a completely different idea about personal space. They stand really close to you when you're talking and you want to move backwards all the time.

Friend: Is that right?

Sarah: Yes, and they don't mind having long silences in their conversations. Every time there was a long pause I wanted to say something. But for them that's quite normal.

Friend: A bit different from here in the States then.

Unit 5, Activity 4: Stress: A modern day disease?

A: Oh yes, I feel quite stressed when I know I'm going to be late for an appointment or for work.

B: So do I. Yesterday I was late leaving for work and then I got stuck in a traffic jam.

C: Yes, and there's nothing you can do. You feel so powerless, don't you?

B: Yes, you do. It's just so frustrating. Especially if every traffic light is red or there's a lot of traffic, so you decide to go another way. And then ... then ... there's even more traffic.

A: Yes, I start looking at my watch about every five seconds.

B: Oh yes, I do that, too.

C: Mm ... yeah. And then you arrive all hot and completely stressed out.

A: And you need a cup of coffee before you start work.

B: Oh yes, I find using the Internet very stressful.

A: Yeah, me too. You type in what you want and then you get thousands of results. You know, you type in a word and it says numbers one to 10 of about 400,000 results. And ... um ... it's always like that.

B: Yes, and sometimes it takes so long to find the information you need, doesn't it?

A: Yes, and that's awful, especially if you're under time pressure.

C: Oh, actually that doesn't bother me so much. But ... but ... I have this really slow Internet connection.

A: Oh yes, ... and...

C: Yeah, and ... anyway, you click on the item you want, then you have to wait and wait until the website appears on the screen. It's so slow.

A: Oh yes. I often start clicking the mouse to make it go more quickly and then ...

B: It stops completely.

A: Yeah, that's right and I get so irritated. I can remember once going into the kitchen and screaming.

B: Oh, that's nothing. My husband once hit the computer.

C: Oh no!

Extra 1, Wales, Activity 2: A week in Wales

Josh: Well, hi there, Dave. I haven't seen you for ages.

David: Oh, hello, Josh. It's nice to see you again after such a long time.

Josh: So how are things?

David: Fine thanks, and you?

Josh: I'm OK, busy as usual. Heh, that's a big bag you have there. Are you going on vacation?

David: Yes, I am. I'm going to Wales for a week to stay with some friends.

Josh: Wales! Sounds great. Where to?

David: To Llanrhaedr-ym-Mochnant near Lake Vyrnwy.

Josh: Oh, no, those Welsh names. To Thlan ... to where?! I can't get my tongue around them.

David: Sorry, I'll try and say that again, slowly. Llanrhaedr-ym-Mochnant.

Josh: You pronounced that well. Ah, but of course David Thomas. Your last name's Thomas. That's a Welsh name, isn't it?

David: Yeah, well ... you know ... my parents come from Wales and they lived in Ruthin. And that's part of so-called "Welsh Wales" – 40% of the people in Ruthin still speak Welsh. So I can speak a little, too.

Josh: Yeah? Rather you than me. I could never pronounce those Welsh names. You aren't related to the great Welsh poet Dylan Thomas, are you?

David: No, I'm not. There just aren't very many Welsh surnames. So if it's not Thomas, it's probably ... um ... Davies, Evans, Williams or Jones. And Jones is the most common name in Wales.

Josh: Oh, is it?

David: Yes, and there's no J in the Welsh language!

Josh: Oh, really, that's interesting. So, ... um .... what about Tom Jones? Is he Welsh?

David: Yes, he is. And so is Catherina Zeta Jones, the actress and .... um Gwyneth Jones.

Josh: Gwyneth Jones? Who's she?

David: She's an opera singer and the other famous Welsh opera singer Bryn Terfel is actually Bryn Terfel Jones.

Josh: Is that right? So ... anyway, what are you doing in Thlan r Mochant? Oh, I remember the first time I went to Wales. Driving around was so confusing. I thought there were two towns on the road signs and actually it was just the Welsh and English name for the same place.

David: Yes, it can be a problem. But, you know, nowadays everything official has to be in Welsh and English, even your electricity and telephone bills and that can be very confusing! That's been the law since ... um ... well, since the early 90s. But anyway ... to get back to your question. I'm going with these friends to the International Eisteddfod in Llangollen.

Josh: Oh, the Eisteddfod! I've heard of that. Isn't that where all the poets and musicians meet – all dressed in strange costumes?

David: No, it isn't, you're thinking of the Royal National Eisteddfod, where they celebrate Welsh culture. This is the International Eisteddfod. It's every July in Llangollen – a lovely little town on the river Dee. Choirs, singers and dancers come from all over the world to take part in contests, but, of course, there are lots of Welsh groups, too.

Josh: Sounds lovely. But I never have much free time in summer.

David: Neither do I. But I always try to go to Llangollen every year.

Josh: Well, perhaps one year I'll join you, but... oh heh look at the time. I'm afraid I must rush back to the office. Duty calls. Say "hi" to Sandra for me. We must all get together soon.

David: Yes, Sandra would love to see you again. I'll give you a ring. Bye.

Unit 7, Activity 2a: Interesting places to live

Tromsø

A: Well, it's a marvellous place. It has the world's northernmost university.

B: Really? I didn't know that.

A: And there's the ocean and the mountains and the fjords are just spectacular.

B: Sounds wonderful, but it is a long way north. I mean, it's a bit cold and dark, isn't it?

A: I know we're 200 kilometres above the Arctic Circle but, actually, the weather is not as bad as you think. Well ... there's a lot of snow of course and the winters are long.

B: Yeah.

A: We sometimes get the first snow in late September and there's not much of a spring. And it's true that you don't often get to wear shorts in summer.

B: And what's it like in winter? It's completely dark, isn't it?

A: Well, the sun only disappears for two months but there's often a grey light in the middle of the day. And all the ski trails are floodlit so it's no problem and the nightlife is pretty good.

B: So you ... um ...

A: Wait, that's not all. The best is still to come. You've forgotten the midnight sun. I mean, have you ever enjoyed a pint of beer in sunshine at one o'clock in the morning?

A: No, I haven't, but I'd love to ...

Alice Springs

C: If you ask me, it's the best place to live in the whole of Australia. Have you ever been in the desert, mate?

D: Well no, I haven't actually.

C: Ah, it's just amazing. So big, so beautiful and just great sunsets.

D: It's a bit isolated though, isn't it?

C: It's OK. It's only about five hours' drive to Uluru. That's Ayers Rock to you. And you can always go to Adelaide if you want a bigger place. That's only about two hours away from Alice Springs.

D: Two hours? By car?

C: No, by plane. Anyway, why would you want to go there? Alice has got everything you need – shops, restaurants, football, water, electricity. You name it, we've got it. We've even got a golf course and the beer's great.

D: Yeah, but what about spiders? I've heard they're poisonous.

C: Ah, they're no problem. I mean, my wife doesn't like them too much. Not the big, hairy ones. And you have to be a bit careful of the Australian Redback but I don't know anyone who's died.

Los Angeles

E: Well, I've been living in LA for just over a year now. And it's a bit of a shock coming from a rural area. There are just so many people. If you count the population of the whole Los Angeles area, then there are over 16 million people.

F: 16 million? I didn't know it was so huge.

E: Yeah, and so getting to work can be a problem. In the rush hour with all that stop and go it can take an hour to get there. And yeah, air pollution can get quite bad in summer sometimes. But I don't go to downtown LA very often. There's no real centre and it's just a concrete jungle.

F: So do you like living in LA?

E: Yeah, it's OK. There are a lot of good things about it – good beaches, mountains, trips to Disneyland and the Hollywood film studios, lots of theatres. There's everything you need if you don't mind travelling. Great weather, too. A lot of blue skies.

F: That sounds wonderful! I particularly like the bit about blue skies.

E: Mm ... yeah ... of course there is a problem with gangs and drugs in some areas but we don't have a problem with crime in our neighborhood.

F: Just earthquakes.

E: Well, yeah, there is a risk of earthquakes and fires and mudslides in the mountains but no one worries about them much.

Unit 7, Selfstudy, Exercise 2: Pronunciation: Certain stressed words

1 I was very sorry to hear that.
2 That's really disappointing.
3 That's too expensive.
4 I quite agree with you.
5 That's rather good.
6 You're so right.

Unit 8, Activity 4: It doesn't work

A: I don't see you at the bus stop very often, Derek.

B: No, well, the car's at the garage, isn't it?

A: What's wrong with it?

B: Well, they're not sure but they think there's something wrong with the electrics. I was in town yesterday and it wouldn't start. In the end I had to ring my wife to come and fetch me.

C: Ah, look, a text message from my sister.

D: Is that a new mobile? What happened to your old one?

C: I dropped it into the washbasin while I was doing my hair.

D: Oh no, you didn't. And it broke, did it?
C: Well, not exactly. I'd just had a wash and the washbasin was still full of water. I know it was really stupid, but ...
D: Well, it's not as bad as me. I put mine on the top of the car and forgot all about it and when I drove off it fell onto the road and smashed.

E: Hello, Peter. How are things?
F: Terrible.
E: Really? Why's that?
F: Oh, the washing machine's broken down. It flooded the bathroom and I've just spent two hours cleaning up.
E: Oh no. I'm sorry to hear that.
F: Yeah, and do you know that's the second thing that's gone wrong this week. The television broke down on Monday.
E: Not the new one you bought.
F: Yeah, we were watching the news on Monday when suddenly we lost the picture. I think it must be faulty. I'll have to go back to the shop and complain.
E: Oh, that's really annoying. You must be really fed up.
F: Yes, I certainly am. Anyway, I'm afraid I've got to go now. There's a man coming to look at the washing machine soon.
E: OK. Bye and good luck.
F: Yeah, bye.

G: Um, Dad, can I borrow your laptop to finish my homework?
H: What's wrong with the computer?
G: Yeah, well ... it's not working.
H: Oh no, it's that damned modem again. That's the third time this month.
G: Dad, I don't think it is the modem. You see, ... I was drinking coffee and I'm afraid I spilt it all over the keyboard.
H: You did what? How many times do I have to tell you not to do that?
G: Yeah, and I think I've deleted some of mum's files, too.
H: Son, she'll kill you.

Unit 9, Activity 3a: Shopping in the States

Pam: In the last seven days? So you mean, since last Friday. Well, on Saturday I went to the supermarket, you know the really huge one on the corner of Queens and Central.
Man: Yeah, I know the one.
Pam: Yeah, well ... I bought all my groceries for the week and I bought some aspirin in there, too. There's a pharmacy and ... um ... oh, yeah, some motor oil And yeah, well actually, that was it.

Pam: Near where I live? Mm ... I don't think I ever go to any of the stores near my house. Oh no, that's not quite true. There's a convenience store I sometimes go to if I've forgotten anything. They're open 24 hours a day.
Man: Oh, right.
Pam: But normally I go to the supermarket or to one of the shopping malls out of town. You can buy everything you need there.

Pam: How often? Oh, I don't go downtown to shop anymore. I mean, I used to go but now most of the stores have moved out of town. And you have to pay for the parking lot downtown and of course you don't have to if you go to the mall.

Pam: Mm ... let me think. From the Internet, mail order catalogues and the TV? Well, I sometimes order things from the Internet. I order books and last month I bought some computer games via the Internet. I like the choice.
Man: Yeah.
Pam: Mail order catalogues – well, I used to buy a lot of clothes from catalogues – pants, blouses and things and my husband sometimes buys sports equipment. And ... er ... what was the last one you said?
Man: TV.
Pam: Oh yeah, TV. No, never ... oh no, that's not quite true. I once bought a clock from one of the shopping channels. But it was a big mistake. It looked good on TV but actually it's quite ugly.

Pam: Mm, actually I like a lot of different kinds of shopping. I like going to the mall. I sometimes spend half a day there. And I just love going to garage sales. Last week my neighbor had one. She's moving to a smaller house and wanted to sell some of her things so I picked up some really good bargains there – a table and some gardening tools.
Man: OK. Is that all?
Pam: Mm, well what's also quite fun is the car show. I always go with my husband.

Pam: Well, yes I do. I don't really like the crowds but I usually go to the pre-Christmas sales at Thanks-giving. I went this year and got all my Christmas cards and a few gifts. And I sometimes go to the summer sales, too.

Pam: Usually by debit card or I use one of my store credit cards. I have one for Macy's and for Walmart.
Man: Yeah, me too.
Pam: Yes, they're useful, aren't they?
Man: Yeah.
Pam: I rarely pay cash. I always have a few dollar bills in my purse for tips and things, but that's it.

Tapescript

Unit 10, Activity 2a: Scary moments

A: Well, I'm in the village band. And last year this French band came over to do a concert with us. And ... um ... anyway, someone had to make a welcome speech and of course I was chosen because I'm the only one who speaks French.

B: Oh, rather you than me. Were you nervous?

A: Yeah, I had a few butterflies in my stomach before the speech but it wasn't too bad. But when I walked into the village hall and saw that there were about 200 people there, I was really frightened.

B: Yeah. So what happened?

A: Well, at first it wasn't too bad. I said something in English and my voice was shaking but it was OK. I even made a joke and everyone laughed.

B: Uhuh.

A: But then I had to say something in French. So I said one or two sentences and suddenly I just had a blank. You know, I forgot the whole speech. I just couldn't think of anything to say.

B: Oh, that's horrible.

A: Yeah, and everyone was looking at me. And my heart started to beat faster and I started to feel faint.

B: Oh, yeah.

A: In the end, I managed to stammer one or two sentences in really bad French but it was so awful.

B: Yeah, I can imagine.

A: Of course everyone was really nice afterwards but I was so embarrassed. Oh, never again.

C: Well, it was my one and only parachute jump.

D: Yeah, well, if you do something stupid like that.

C: Yeah, I know. I did a tandem jump.

D: A tandem jump? What's that?

C: That's when you do the jump attached to the flying instructor. You free fall for about 30 seconds before the instructor opens the parachute.

D: OK. Yeah.

C: Well, in the morning we had a short training course and in the afternoon we did the parachute jump. So we got into the plane and at first I felt fine. You know, I was enjoying the view. But then as we got higher and higher I started feeling quite nervous. I started sweating and was a bit short of breath.

D: Oh dear.

C: Yeah and after that I couldn't even look out of the window. In fact, when it was time to jump I was absolutely terrified. I didn't want to do the jump at all and my legs were shaking so much that I found it difficult to stand up.

D: So did you do it?

C: Yeah, in the end they persuaded me – they told me how wonderful it is and everything and so I said OK. Anyway, we jumped and, you'll never guess what happened ...

D: What?

C: I fainted.

D: Fainted?

C: Yeah, yeah, I fainted and the next thing I knew we were landing.

D: So you missed it?

C: Yeah, I came round just before the landing.

Unit 12, Activity 2a: Learning experiences

John: I met Mr Butcher last week. Can you remember him?

Karen: Mr Butcher? Ah, he was the one who taught us history. Oh, I remember. He was the one who was incredibly boring.

John: Yes, I remember when Susan once fell asleep in his lesson and he didn't even notice.

Karen: Yeah, and he always shouted at me because of my bad handwriting.

John: Oh yes, he hated bad handwriting. Mine was terrible, too.

Karen: I mean, I really tried to write nicely but I just couldn't. Actually it's still awful. It hasn't improved at all. In fact, I think it's even worse now.

John: Is it? So is mine. I expect no one shouts at you about it though.

Karen: No, that's true. You know, I was looking through some old photo albums yesterday and found some photos of that wonderful class trip to France. It was the first time I went abroad. That's something I'll never forget. I don't think our French improved though.

John: Yes, I can remember trying to order a coke and getting a cup of coffee instead.

Karen: Oh, yes, that's right. Yeah, those were the days. So ... um ... what are you doing now? Didn't you want to be a baker or a chef, or something?

John: Yes, I did, a chef – but my parents said I had to work in a bank. So I went to work in a bank. And I hated it. I was always terrible at maths. My worst subject! I always got low marks.

Karen: Not the right skills for a bank clerk then.

John: No, certainly not. I'll never forget the first banking exams I took. I can remember turning over the page and looking at the questions and from the 12 questions – or however many there were – I could only answer one. I was so embarrassed when I got my exam results and I got a D. D for dreadful.

Karen: So are you still at the bank?

John: No, I'm not. I refused to continue and in the end my mother let me do an apprenticeship as a chef.

Karen: Oh, good for you.

John: So, what about you? What did you do?

Karen: Well, I started as a dental assistant but didn't really enjoy it. Anyway, when the kids were small I did a part-time computer course at Avon community college. You know, the one in town.

And then later I retrained and did a full-time course in social work. At the same college.

John: Yeah.

Karen: I'm much happier as a social worker than I was as a dental assistant.

John: Oh, that's good.

Karen: Oh, look, everyone's leaving.

John: The time's really flown by.

Karen: Are you coming for coffee tomorrow? Everyone's meeting at Susan's house.

John: Oh no, I've got my last sailing lesson.

Karen: Oh, you're learning to sail.

John: Yes, I'm really enjoying it. It's one of the nicest things I've ever done. I wish I'd done it earlier. I just love being on the water. It's so peaceful. There's just you and the wind. And to my surprise I'm really good at it.

Karen: Sounds great!

John: Anyway, it's been great talking to you again.

Karen: Yes, see you again in five years.

Extra 2, Eastern Canada, Activity 2: A TV Programme

Mike: Did you see that programme on TV last night – the one on eastern Canada?

Laura: Yes, I did actually. It even showed St John's in Newfoundland. That's where I grew up.

Kevin: Oh, I didn't watch it. Was it good?

Mike: Yes, it was really interesting. I didn't realise what an amazing country Canada is. I mean, it's just huge.

Laura: Yeah, and it's almost empty compared to Europe. There are only about 22 million living in the east.

Mike: And ... you know ... what I found really fascinating was that two-thirds of the country is undeveloped – there are only forests and lakes and bears and beavers and things. Parts of the country are almost impossible to reach and the distances are just incredible.

Laura: Yeah, it takes nine hours to fly from the east Coast to the west coast. It even takes three hours to fly from St John's to Toronto. It's not something you do very often.

Kevin: That's the capital, isn't it?

Laura: No, that's Ottawa. Toronto is the largest city in Canada.

Kevin: Have you been there?

Laura: Yeah, I have. It's a wonderful place. It's ... um ...

Mike: Yes, they showed Toronto ... Oh sorry. I interrupted you. Do go on.

Laura: Oh, I just wanted to say that it's really multi-cultural. There are about 100 nationalities living there. I think in Ontario over a quarter of the people were born outside of Canada.

Kevin: Oh, really? So are there a lot of problems?

Laura: No, it's not too bad. Canada is a country of immigrants. And most people are accepted. Well, as long as they mow their front lawns, of course. You know, it's very important that the front gardens look tidy.

Mike: I thought that Toronto looked really interesting. They showed Chinatown and Little Italy and they have a Caribbean festival every year.

Laura: Yeah, that's right and further west there's a place called Kitchener where all the German immigrants settled. They even have an Oktoberfest.

Kevin: I didn't know there were so many Germans there.

Laura: Yeah, it's the third largest group after the British and the French.

Mike: Uhuh, then there are the Mennonites.

Kevin: The Mennonites?

Mike: Those are the people who still use horses instead of cars and don't have any electricity. And you have to imagine how cold the winters are, apparently even in the south the temperatures can drop to –30 and there are blizzards. Brr.

Laura: Well, I think it's not quite so cold where they live, but in the south of Quebec temperatures of –20 are quite normal in winter. But you get used to it.

Mike: Well, if you ask me, –20 is far too cold.

Kevin: And just imagine the Eskimos in their igloos.

Laura: They don't live in igloos anymore. They have proper houses and televisions and the Internet.

Mike: Ah, did you know the word Eskimo means eater of raw meat? They prefer to be called Inuit.

Laura: And you call the Indians the First Nations.

Mike: Oh, that Pow Wow of the Iroquois they showed was great, wasn't it? I'd really like to go to one.

Kevin: It sounds really good.

Mike: Actually, Canada must be a really interesting place to live. Although I'm not sure I'd like to live in Quebec. My French is terrible.

Kevin: But aren't they bilingual?

Laura: No, only a few of them are. They're mostly French speakers and some of them can't speak any English at all. I mean, you really have to speak French in Quebec. They definitely have their own French culture. They're a bit different from the rest of Canada.

Mike: Yeah, they said that French was the second official language and I think over 80% of people in Quebec have French as their mother tongue.

Kevin: Oh yes, didn't they have a referendum for an independent Quebec?

Laura: Yeah, and it was a really close vote. Nearly half the people who voted, voted for independence.

Mike: Anyway, I thought Canada was a great place.

Kevin: So do you want to move there?

Laura: He can't move there. He'd miss the football. Ice hockey is our most popular game.

Mike: And have you seen me on skates?

Grammar check

1 Überblick über die Zeiten / Summary of verb tenses

Die wichtigsten Zeitformen im Englischen sind: die Gegenwart, die vollendete Gegenwart und die Vergangenheit. Bei jeder Zeitform (*tense*) im Englischen gibt es zwei *aspects*: die einfache Form (simple form) und die Verlaufsform (progressive form bzw. –ing form). Die Darstellung der Verbformen in der nachstehenden Übersicht soll die Bildung der Zeitformen und die logische Reihenfolge verdeutlichen.

Vergangenheit	Vollendete Gegenwart	Gegenwart
simple x	simple x	simple x
past		**present**
I worked very hard.	I have worked very hard.	I work very hard.
Did you work very hard?	Have you worked hard?	Do you work very hard?
No, I didn't.	No, I haven't.	No, I don't.
progressive	progressive	progressive
I was working very hard.	I have been working very hard.	I am working very hard.
Were you working very hard?	Have you been working hard?	Are you working hard?
No, I wasn't.	No, I haven't.	No, I'm not.

Das Symbol x drückt entweder eine Tatsache oder eine Handlung bzw. mehrere Handlungen aus.
Die Linie symbolisiert den für die –ing-Form charakteristischen Ablauf einer Handlung.

1a Vervollständigen Sie nun die folgenden Aussagen mit: *be*, *do*, oder *have*

In der einfachen Form der Vergangenheit und Gegenwart werden Frage und Verneinung mit einer Form von .... gebildet . Im Gegensatz dazu werden die Verlaufsformen mit einer Form von .... und einem Verb mit der Endung *–ing* gebildet. Die vollendete Gegenwart wird mit .... und dem Mittelwort der Vergangenheit (Partizip Perfekt) gebildet und stellt eine Art Zeitbrücke zwischen Vergangenheit und Gegenwart dar.

1b Welche Zeitangabe passt am besten zu den folgenden Zeitformen? Ergänzen Sie die Sätze mit folgenden Wörtern und Wendungen: *in 2001 / when / never / on Mondays / the last two years / today*

1 I usually work late ....
2 I'm working on a new project ....
3 I have been working for my boss for ....
4 I've .... worked for a large company.
5 I worked in the travel agency for two months ....
6 I was working at the travel agent's .... I met my husband.

2 Die Gegenwart (einfache Form und Verlaufsform) / The simple present and present progressive U1 / R S.12

1 ☐ Die einfache Gegenwart wird verwendet, um allgemeine Tatsachen zu beschreiben.
2 ☐ Die einfache Gegenwart bezeichnet gewohnheitsmäßige, sich wiederholende Handlungen.
3 ☐ Die Verlaufsform der Gegenwart beschreibt gerade ablaufende bzw. vorübergehende Handlungen.
4 ☐ Die Verlaufsform der Gegenwart mit zukünftiger Bedeutung drückt bereits festgelegte Pläne aus.

U = Unit, R = Remember und S = Seite

2a Ordnen Sie die Sätze den Erklärungen in Übung 2 zu.

a) We're flying to Paris in May.
b) Germans don't watch as much television as the British.
c) David's talking to his mother on the phone.
d) I always do the housework on Saturdays.

2b Setzen Sie die Verben in die einfache oder Verlaufsform der Gegenwart.

I (1) .... (have) terrible problems with my daughter Jane at the moment. You know, she (2) .... (not do) well at school. She (3) .... (get) homework every day but she simply (4) .... (refuse) to do it. She (5) .... (watch) television most afternoons and (6) .... (not listen) to what I say. She (7) .... (take) her school leaving exams in two months' time so I'm really very worried.

3 Die Vergangenheit (einfache Form und Verlaufsform) / The simple past and past progressive U3 / R S. 20

1 ☐ Die **einfache Vergangenheit** wird für Einzelhandlungen verwendet, die in der Vergangenheit abgeschlossen wurden.
2 ☐ Die **einfache Vergangenheit** wird auch für eine abgeschlossene Reihe von Einzelhandlungen verwendet.
3 ☐ Die **einfache Vergangenheit** bezeichnet Handlungen, die sich in der Vergangenheit mehrmals bzw. regelmäßig wiederholten.
4 ☐ Die **Verlaufsform der Vergangenheit** beschreibt eine Handlung, die bereits im Gange war, als eine neue hinzukam oder diese unterbrach.
5 ☐ Die **Verlaufsform der Vergangenheit** wird verwendet, um etwas zu beschreiben, das zu einem Zeitpunkt in der Vergangenheit gerade ablief.

3a Ordnen Sie die Sätze den obigen Erklärungen zu.

a) The train was just coming into the station when his mobile rang.
b) They visited the Taj Mahal last summer.
c) It was midday and the sun was shining.
d) His parents always went to Spain for their holidays.
e) They walked out of the station, got on the bus and sat down behind the driver.

3b Streichen Sie die Zeitformen, die nicht richtig sind.

Marc usually drives to work when the weather is bad. Last Friday it (1) *rained / was raining* quite hard so he (2) *went / was going* to work by car. He (3) *was driving / drove* down a country road when suddenly he (4) *noticed / was noticing* a man lying at the side of the road. He stopped the car and (5) *got out / was getting out*. He realised immediately that the man needed help and (6) *was phoning / phoned* for an ambulance. His quick thinking saved the man's life.

4 Die vollendete Gegenwart / The present perfect U4 / R S. 22, U11 / R S. 55

Die **vollendete Gegenwart (einfache Form)** wird verwendet:

1 ☐ wenn es nicht wichtig ist, wann etwas geschehen ist, sondern **dass es** überhaupt **geschah**.
2 ☐ wenn **Zustände** in der Vergangenheit begonnen haben und bis in die Gegenwart hineinreichen.
3 ☐ wenn **Dinge mehrmals** bis zum heutigen Zeitpunkt geschehen sind. Das **Endergebnis** wird betont.
4 ☐ auch mit **ever**, **never**, wenn sich die Zeitspanne auf das gesamte Leben einer Person bis zum heutigen Zeitpunkt bezieht.

Grammar check

4a Ordnen Sie die folgenden Sätze den Erklärungen in Übung 4 zu.

a) I've stayed at that hotel three times.
b) She's been on a cruise.
c) They've never been to an English-speaking country.
d) I have known George for many years.

Die Verlaufsform der vollendeten Gegenwart / The present perfect progressive U7 / R S. 40

Die Verlaufsform der vollendeten Gegenwart wird verwendet, wenn Handlungen in der Vergangenheit begonnen haben und in der Gegenwart noch andauern sowie wenn man den Zeitraum bzw. die Dauer einer Handlung betonen will: *I've been working in the garden all morning and there's still so much to do.*

4b Verwenden Sie die einfache Form oder Verlaufsform der vollendeten Gegenwart in folgenden Sätzen.

1 I .... (look for) a house all summer but I haven't found anything yet.
2 We .... (drive) round this area since early this morning, but so far have had no luck.
3 Up to now we .... (look at) over 20 houses altogether.
4 You .... (never, see) so many awful places.
5 Now we .... (decide) to stay in our own house after all.

Zeitangaben in der vollendeten Gegenwart (seit) / The present perfect with *since* and *for* U7 / R S. 40

seit

since
● Zeitpunkt

for
〰➤ Zeitdauer

genaue Angabe des Zeitpunkts einer Handlung bzw. eines Ereignisses in der Vergangenheit (seit dem eine Handlung andauert)

since 10 o'clock
since Tuesday
since March
since 2000
since I was born

Angabe der Zeitdauer meist durch eine Konstruktion mit a/an bzw. einem Hauptwort im Plural (-s).

for a week
for an hour
for ten days
for many years
for ages

4c Ergänzen Sie die folgenden Sätze mit *since* and *for*. Schreiben Sie in die Kästchen entweder (•) Zeitpunkt oder (〰➤) Zeitdauer um die Begriffe zu verdeutlichen.

1 He's been sitting in this chair .... he came in. ☐
.... over six hours. ☐
.... 9 o'clock. ☐

2 They've been living in the house .... a long time. ☐
.... 1988. ☐
.... over 30 years. ☐

5 Die Zukunft mit *going to* / The future with *going to* U9 / R S. 48

Um **Absichten** oder **vorher überlegte Pläne** für die Zukunft auszudrücken, verwendet man ***going to***.

5a Verwenden Sie *going to*, um folgende Sätze zu ergänzen.

"What .... you and Steve .... (do) for your birthday ?"

"We .... (invite) some friends round for a meal. But I .... (not cook). Steve .... (order) the food from our local Italian retaurant and we .... (enjoy) entertaining our friends at home without spending the whole day in the kitchen."

6 Die Zukunft mit *will* / The future with *will* U10 / R S. 52

Die **Zukunft mit *will*** wird für **allgemeine Aussagen** über die Zukunft sowie für **Vorhersagen** und **Vermutungen** verwendet.

6a Ergänzen Sie die Sätze mit *have to, improve, live, suffer from, work.*

1 By 2020 a third of the population .... from home.

2 Next semester students .... pay higher tuition fees.

3 Doctors say that in future more and more people .... allergies.

4 Progress in medicine means that people .... longer.

5 I'm sure the health service .... a lot.

Nach **Verben** wie *think, hope, expect* und *know* wird häufig die **Zukunft mit *will*** verwendet.

6b Ordnen Sie die Aussagen (1-4) den Reaktionen (a-d) zu.

1 Ron isn't here yet.
2 It's his first flight.
3 Look what I've bought for him.
4 Do you think we'll ever get there?

☐ a) I hope he won't be scared.
☐ b) Do you think it will be useful?
☐ c) Don't worry, I know we will. We'll have a great time.
☐ d) I expect he'll arrive late as usual.

7 *If*-Sätze Typ 1 und Typ 2 / Conditional sentences: First conditional / second conditional U2 / R S. 16

If I **stay** at home, I **will** have to give up my career.

***If*-Sätze Typ 1** drücken aus, welche Folge es für die Zukunft hat, wenn in der Gegenwart etwas geschieht oder nicht geschieht.

If I **stayed** at home, I **would** have to give up my career.

***If*-Sätze Typ 2** beschreiben eine Situation, die als solche nicht existiert, die aber vorstellbar ist.

7a Welche Aussage, a) oder b), beschreibt am besten *If*-Sätze von Typ 1 bzw. Typ 2?

a) Typ ☐ beschreibt eine theoretische Überlegung. b) Typ ☐ beschreibt eine konkrete Situation.

7b Ergänzen Sie die Sätze mit *will* oder *would*.

1 It .... probably cause problems if your mother-in-law comes to live with you.

2 If you moved into our neighbourhood, your children .... be near a good school.

3 .... you emigrate to Canada if they offer you the job?

4 If you found a house near your work, ... you buy it?

8 Mengenangaben / *a lot of – lots of – much – many* U5 / R S. 26

A lot of und *lots of* werden sehr häufig gebraucht. Sie bedeuten sowohl *viel* als auch *viele* und werden in normalen Aussagesätzen, in verneinten Sätzen und in Fragen benutzt. *Much* (viel) und *many* (viele) werden hauptsächlich in folgenden Fällen verwendet:

- in verneinten Sätzen
- in Fragen
- nach *very*, *so*, *too* und *how*

8a Ergänzen Sie folgende Sätze mit *a lot of*, *much* und *many*.

1 People buy .... convenience food.

2 We eat far too .... food.

3 Office workers don't usually get .... / .... exercise. (zwei Möglichkeiten)

4 They don't really have so .... opportunities for taking exercise.

5 How .... free time do they have?

6 How .... hours do you sleep each night?

7 Can you find .... / .... good advice on special diets on the Internet? (zwei Möglichkeiten)

9 Eigenschaftswörter (erste und zweite Steigerungsstufe) / Adjectives (comparatives and superlatives) U6 / R S. 32

9a Ergänzen Sie folgende Tabelle. Bei jedem Eigenschaftswort *(adjective)* fehlt eine Form.

	Eigenschafts-wort/Adjektiv	1. Steigerungsform / Komparativ	2. Steigerungsform / Superlativ
1 Einsilbige Adjektive	keen	keener	(the) ______
	cheap	______	(the) cheapest
1a Einsilbige Adjektive mit d, g, t usw. am Ende: Verdoppelung, wenn ein kurzer Vokal vorausgeht	big	______	(the) biggest
	fit	fitter	(the) ______
2 Zweisilbige Adjektive, die auf *-le -er*, *-ow* oder *-y* enden (Das *-y* am Ende wird zu *-i-*)	clever	______	(the) cleverest
	healthy	healthier	(the) ______
2a Andere zweisilbige Adjektive	famous	______	(the) most famous
	useful	more useful	(the) ______ useful
3 Adjektive mit drei oder mehr Silben	dangerous	more dangerous	(the) ______
	interesting	______	(the) most interesting

Ausnahmen: good, better, the best; bad, worse, the worst; little, less, the least.

So werden Vergleiche ausgedrückt: He is fitter **than** me. (als) I'm not **as** fit **as** I used to be. (so ... wie)

9b Ergänzen Sie die Sätze. Achten Sie auf den Gebrauch von *as* und *than*.

1 In Britain a visit to the pub is the .... leisure time activity. (common)

2 Nowadays it's .... to find a pub that serves meals .... it used to be. (easy)

3 Opening hours in British pubs are now .... than they were 20 years ago. (flexible)

4 The lounge bar is .... than the public bar. (comfortable)

5 Pub crawling is as .... with young women .... it is with young men. (popular)

6 The .... place to meet British people is in a pub. (good)

10 Umstandswörter / Adverbs of manner U12 / R S. 58

Umstandswörter stehen nach dem Verb und beschreiben die Tätigkeit genauer.
Die meisten Umstandswörter werden durch Anhängen von **–ly** an das Adjektiv gebildet: quick / quick**ly**.

10a Streichen Sie die Wörter, die in den Sätzen nicht verwendet werden können. Achten Sie auf manche unregelmäßige Adverbien.

1 She sang the aria *beautifully / well / excellent.*
2 He speaks three languages *good / perfectly / fluently.*
3 They both work very *hard / hardly / quickly.*
4 He drove very *badly / bad / fast.*
5 She welcomed us *friendly / warmly / enthusiastically.*

11 Früher / *used to* U8 / R S. 44

Die Wendung ***used to*** wird für Handlungen verwendet, die man **in der Vergangenheit zu tun pflegte**, die in der Gegenwart jedoch nicht mehr stattfinden.

11a Bilden Sie Sätze mit *used to / did you use to? / didn't use to*

1 He exercises on his rowing machine every day now. He .... (do) any exercise at all.

2 I put everything in the washing machine these days. I .... (wash) my silk blouses by hand.

3 What .... you .... (do) in the evenings before you bought the TV?

12 Gerund und Infinitv / gerund and infinitive U3 / R S. 20

Das **Gerund** ist streng genommen ein **Substantiv**, das aus einer Verbform gebildet wird. Vergleichen Sie *I like the **ferry**, but I hate the **tunnel*** (*like* plus **Substantiv**) mit *I like **taking** the ferry, but I hate **using** the tunnel* (*like* plus **Gerundium**).
Eine Reihe von Verben wird mit dem Gerundium und nicht mit dem Infinitiv (wie im Deutschen) verbunden: *love, like, dislike, enjoy, hate, prefer, can't stand, don't mind* usw.
Wenn jedoch die Verben *love, like, hate* und *prefer* mit ***would*** gebildet werden, folgt der **Infinitiv**, z.B. *I'd love to spend a few weeks in the country.*

12a **Gerund** oder **Infinitiv**? Ergänzen Sie die Lücken mit *drive*.

1 Joan still enjoys .... although she is nearly eighty.

2 But she wouldn't like .... an automatic because she is not used to it.

3 This summer she'd love .... to Scotland with a friend, but it's a long journey.

4 She hates .... on the motorways.

p. 79

Dictionary

Hier finden Sie neue Wörter und Wendungen von *English Network Basic Conversation* in alphabetischer Reihenfolge mit ihrer phonetischen Umschrift und ihrer deutschen Übersetzung.

Die Fundstellen sind folgendermaßen zu lesen: Die erste Ziffer bezeichnet die Unit. Die daran anschließende Ziffer gibt die Übungsnummer an. Der Zusatz SS verweist auf die Selfstudy-Seite der entsprechenden Unit. Damit finden Sie *raise* (2.4) in Unit 2 / Activity 4, *hoover* (1.SS.3) auf der *Selfstudy*-Seite von Unit 1.
Außerdem gibt es folgende Abkürzungen: GS: *Getting Started*, T: *Tip*, LC: *Language & Culture*, TV: *Topic Vocabulary*, K: *Key*. Die Wörter, die in den *Extras* auftauchen, sind mit E1 und E2 bezeichnet.

Phonetische Lautschrift

englischer Laut		ähnlicher deutscher Laut	englischer Laut		ähnlicher deutscher Laut
[ɪ]	in	*in*	[ɪə]	here	*hier*
[e]	yes	*fett*	[eə]	where	*sehr*
[æ]	thanks	zwischen *a* und *ä*	[ʊə]	tourist	[ʊ] + [ə]
[ʌ]	come	*machen*	[v]	have	*Virus*
[ɒ]	coffee	*Motte*	[θ]	thanks	wie ein gelispeltes *ss* in *Biss*
[ʊ]	look	*Butter*	[ð]	this	wie ein gelispeltes *s* in *Sand*
[ə]	number	*singe*	[s]	seat	*Muße*
[iː]	meet	*Knie*	[z]	please	*Museum*
[ɑː]	father	*Bahn*	[ʃ]	she	*Schiff*
[ɔː]	four	wie *o* in deutsch *Borke*	[ʒ]	television	*Regie*
[uː]	too	*Buch*	[tʃ]	cheers	*klatschen*
[ɜː]	early	*Börse*	[dʒ]	German	[d] + [ʒ]
[eɪ]	day	nicht wie deutsch *ei* sondern [e] + [ɪ]	[ŋ]	song	*singen*
[aɪ]	nice	*Eile*	[l]	old	hinten im Mund gesprochen
[ɔɪ]	boy	*heute*	[j]	unit	*ja*
[aʊ]	how	*Frau*	[w]	we	durch die Lippen gesprochen wie [uː]
[əʊ]	no	[ə] + [ʊ]	[r]	repeat	vorn im Mund gesprochen

[ː] der vorangehende Laut wird lang gesprochen
['] Hauptbetonung: die folgende Silbe wird stark betont
[ˌ] Nebenbetonung: die folgende Silbe wird leicht betont

A

accidentally [ˌæksɪ'dentlɪ] versehentlich, zufällig 1.LC
accommodation [əˌkɒmə'deɪʃən]: **self-catering accommodation** Unterkunft für Selbstversorger 4.TV
account [ə'kaʊnt] Gespräch 10.SS.2
account for [ə'kaʊnt fə] ausmachen 4.LC
achieve [ə'tʃiːv] erreichen 2.TV
acquaintance [ə'kweɪntəns] Bekanntschaft; Bekannte/r 2.TV
activity [æk'tɪvətɪ] *hier:* Veranstaltung 7.3b
adapt to [ə'dæpt‿tə] sich anpassen an, sich gewöhnen an 4.TV
addicted [ə'dɪktəd] abhängig, süchtig, 6.5
admire [əd'maɪə] bewundern 2.4
adolescence [ˌædə'lesəns] Jugend 11.1a
adolescent [ˌædə'lesənt] Heranwachsende/r, Jugendliche/r 5.LC
adult education centre [ˌædʌlt‿edjʊ'keɪʃən ˌsentə] Volkshochschule 12.TV
adulthood ['ædʌlthʊd] Erwachsensein, Erwachsenenalter 11.5
Advent wreath ['ædvənt ˌriːθ] Adventskranz 12.1
adventurous [əd'ventʃərəs] abenteuerlich, gewagt E1.3
affect [ə'fekt] beeinflussen, sich auswirken auf 1.6
after all [ˌɑːftər‿'ɔːl] schließlich, letzten Endes, also doch 8.SS.2
again [ə'gen]: **every now and again** ab und zu, dann und wann 1.TV
agreement [ə'griːmənt] Zustimmung 5.2a
aid [eɪd]: **first aid** erste Hilfe 12.1
air hostess ['eə ˌhəʊstəs] Stewardess 10.LC
airsick ['eəˌsɪk] luftkrank 3.SS.3
alarm clock [ə'lɑːm klɒk] Wecker 1.1
alive [ə'laɪv] lebendig, am Leben E2.4
all [ɔːl]: **after all** schließlich, letzten Endes, also doch 8.SS.2
almost ['ɔːlməʊst] fast, beinahe GS.5a
amazing [ə'meɪzɪŋ] erstaunlich, fantastisch, toll 4.4
and so on [ˌænd səʊ‿'ɒn] und so weiter E2.4
annoyed [ə'nɔɪd] ärgerlich, verärgert 5.TV
anxious ['æŋkʃəs] besorgt 5.4
apart from [ə'pɑːt frəm] abgesehen von GS.5a
apparently [ə'pærəntlɪ] offensichtlich, scheinbar 3.4
appeal to [ə'piːl tə] ansprechen, gefallen 6.LC
apply to [ə'plaɪ tə] gelten für, zutreffen auf 5.1
apprenticeship [ə'prentɪsʃɪp] Ausbildung, Lehre 12.2a
approach [ə'prəʊtʃ] Einstellung 2.TV
area ['eərɪə]: **industrial area** Industriegebiet, Gewerbegebiet 7.TV; **residential area** Wohngebiet, Wohngegend 7.TV
art [ɑːt]: **fine art** schöne Künste E2.4
Artic Circle [ˌɑːktɪk 'sɜːkəl] Polarkreis 7.2a
as [əz]: **as a matter of fact** in der Tat, tatsächlich 9.1; **as soon as** sobald 1.1

asleep [ə'sli:p]: **fall asleep** einschlafen 3.4
assembly [ə'semblɪ] Versammlung E1.1
assistant [ə'sɪstənt]: **dental assistant** Zahnarzthelfer/in 12.2a
associate with [ə'səʊʃɪeɪt wɪð] in Verbindung bringen mit E1.K
attendant [əˌtendənt]: **flight attendant** Flugbegleiter/in 10.LC
attention [ə'tenʃən]: **pay attention to** Aufmerksamkeit schenken, beachten 1.4b
attitude ['ætɪtju:d] Haltung, Einstellung 10.LC
authentic [ɔ:'θentɪk] authentisch, echt 7.SS.2
auxiliary [ɔ:g'zɪljərɪ] Hilfsverb 3.2a
average ['ævərɪdʒ]: **on average** im Durchschnitt 1.1
avoid doing s.th. [a'vɔɪd_ˌdu:ɪŋ ˌsʌmθɪŋ] es vermeiden, etw. zu tun 10.LC

B

back up file ['bæk_ʌp ˌfaɪl] Sicherungskopie 8.TV
backwards ['bækwədz] zurück, nach hinten 4.4
baggy ['bægɪ] ausgebeult; sackartig herabhängend; weit 11.SS.3
bagpipe ['bægpaɪp] Dudelsack E2.4
baker ['beɪkə] Bäcker/in 12.2a
balance ['bæləns]: **bank balance** Kontostand 9.1
ballroom dancing [ˌbɔ:lrʊm 'dɑ:nsɪŋ] Gesellschaftstanz 6.TV
bank [bæŋk]: **bank balance** Kontostand 9.1; **bank loan** Bankdarlehen, Bankkredit 9.1; **bank transfer** Überweisung 9.TV
bar [bɑ:]: **lounge bar** *der vornehmere Teil eines Pubs mit eigener Bar* 6.LC; **public bar** Ausschank, Schänke 6.LC; **bar of chocolate** Tafel Schokolade, Schokoladenriegel 5.2a
bargain ['bɑ:gɪn] Schnäppchen, Sonderangebot 9.4b
bark [bɑ:k] bellen 1.3
bath [bɑ:θ]: **soak in the bath** lange in der Wanne liegen 6.5; **bath salts** Badesalz 6.5
Bavaria [bə'veərɪə] Bayern GS.5a
bay [beɪ] Bucht E1.3
be [bi:]: **be in control of** unter Kontrolle haben 3.TV; **be in good/bad shape** in guter/schlechter Verfassung sein 5.TV; **be in good/poor health** in/bei guter/schlechter Gesundheit sein 5.TV; **be on a diet** eine Diät machen 5.2a; **be spoilt for choice** die Qual der Wahl haben 4.LC; **be well worth a visit** sehr wohl einen Besuch wert sein E1.3

beach [bi:tʃ]: **on the beach** am Strand 4.TV
beaver ['bi:və] Biber E2.4
beggar ['begə] Bettler/in 9.LC
behaviour [bɪ'heɪvjə] Verhalten 10.LC
below [bɪ'ləʊ] unten 11.1b
belt [belt] Gürtel 11.TV
bilingual [baɪ'lɪŋgwəl] zweisprachig E2.4
blank [blæŋk]: **have a blank** *(informal)* einen Blackout haben 10.2a; **My mind went blank.** *(informal)* Ich hatte einen Blackout. GS.5a
bless [bles] segnen 4.4
blizzard ['blɪzəd] Blizzard, heftiger Schneesturm 7.TV
blow about/away [ˌbləʊ_ə'baʊt/ə'weɪ] umher-, wegwehen 10.SS.1
board games *(pl.)* ['bɔ:d geɪmz] Brettspiele 6.TV
boarding school ['bɔ:dɪŋ sku:l] Internat 12.TV
boiling ['bɔɪlɪŋ] siedend, kochend 4.4
bold [bəʊld] fett (gedruckt) 2.SS.2
border ['bɔ:də] Grenze 7.TV
bored [bɔ:d]: **get bored** sich langweilen 12.SS.3
bother ['bɒðə] ärgern, stören 5.4
brave [breɪv] tapfer, mutig GS.5a
breath [breθ] Atem 10.2a; **short of breath** außer Atem, kurzatmig 5.TV
breathing ['bri:ðɪŋ] Atmung 5.SS.1
breathtaking ['breθˌteɪkɪŋ] atemberaubend 4.TV
breeding ground ['bri:dɪŋ ˌgraʊnd] Brutstätte, Brutplatz E1.3
bridal ['braɪdl] Braut-, bräutlich 2.LC; **bridal shower** *Brautparty, bei der Geschenke überreicht werden* 2.LC
bride [braɪd] Braut 2.LC
bring along [ˌbrɪŋ_ə'lɒŋ] mitbringen 2.LC
builder ['bɪldə] Erbauer/in E2.3
bump into ['bʌmp_ˌɪntə] zusammenstoßen mit 1.LC
burst [bɜ:st] explodieren *(fig.)* E2.4
butterflies ['bʌtəflaɪs]: **have butterflies in one's stomach** das Flattern haben 10.2a
button ['bʌtn]: **snooze button** Schlummertaste 1.1; **pause button** Pausentaste 5.SS.2b
by this time [ˌbaɪ ðɪs 'taɪm] *hier:* inzwischen, mittlerweile 3.4

C

cage [keɪdʒ] Käfig; Aufzugskabine E1.3
calculator ['kælkjʊleɪtə] Rechner 8.TV
call [kɔ:l]: **local call** Ortsgespräch 8.TV; **long-distance call** Ferngespräch 8.TV; **urgent call** dringendes Gespräch 8.TV

call [kɔ:l]: **call after** benennen nach GS.1; **duty calls** die Pflicht ruft E1.2
caller ['kɔ:lə] Anrufer 2.2a
calm [kɑ:m] ruhig, gelassen 10.1b
cancel ['kænsəl] absagen, kündigen 5.SS.2a
canoe [kə'nu:] paddeln E2.4
canoeing [kə'nu:ɪŋ] Kanufahren 6.3
canoeist [kə'nu:ɪst] Kanute/Kanutin E2.4
card [kɑ:d]: **debit card** *Bankkarte mit Sofortabbuchungsfunktion (z. B. EC-Karte)* 9.3a; **store credit card** Kundenkarte 9.3a
careful ['keəfəl] vorsichtig, sorgfältig 4.4
carpenter ['kɑ:pəntə] Tischler, Zimmerer, Zimmermann 12.TV
carpet ['kɑ:pɪt] Teppich, Teppichboden 8.2
carry on [ˌkærɪ_'ɒn] weitermachen 6.3
carsick ['kɑ:ˌsɪk] autokrank 3.2b
cash [kæʃ]: **pay cash** bar zahlen 9.1
catch up with [kætʃ_'ʌp wɪð] einholen, *hier:* auf dem Laufenden sein 9.LC
cell phone ['sel ˌfəʊn] Mobiltelefon, Handy 8.SS.2
centre ['sentə]: **adult education centre** Volkshochschule 12.TV; **shopping centre** Einkaufszentrum 9.3a
challenge ['tʃælɪndʒ] Herausforderung, Aufgabe 2.5
changeable ['tʃeɪndʒəbəl] unbeständig, wechselhaft 7.TV
channel ['ʃɒpɪŋ ˌtʃænl]: **shopping channel** Einkaufsfernsehen 9.3a
chapel ['tʃæpəl] Kapelle E1.3
chemistry ['kemɪstrɪ] Chemie 12.TV
cherry ['tʃerɪ] Kirsche GS.5a
chewing gum ['tʃu:ɪŋ ˌgʌm] Kaugummi 5.5
chocolate ['tʃɒklət]: **bar of chocolate** Tafel Schokolade, Schokoladenriegel 5.2a
choice [tʃɔɪs] (Aus)Wahl 10.SS.2; **be spoilt for choice** die Qual der Wahl haben 4.LC
choir ['kwaɪə] Chor E1.2
chopsticks *(pl.)* ['tʃɒpstɪks] Essstäbchen 4.4
chords *(pl.)* [kɔ:dz]: **vocal chords** *(pl.)* Stimmbänder 2.SS.2
Circle ['sɜ:kəl]: **Artic Circle** Polarkreis 7.2a
citizen ['sɪtɪzən]: **senior citizen** Senior/in 2.TV
class [klɑ:s]: **evening classes** *(pl.)* Abendkurse 12.TV
class [klɑ:s] einordnen, klassifizieren 5.LC
cleaner ['kli:nə]: **vacuum cleaner** Staubsauger 8.TV
click on ['klɪk_ɒn] anklicken 5.4
cliff [klɪf] Felsen, Klippe E1.3
climb [klaɪm] Klettersteig E1.3
climb [klaɪm] klettern 11.3

Dictionary

clock [klɒk]: **alarm clock** Wecker 1.1
close friend [ˌkləʊs 'frend] enge/r Freund/in 2.1
coach [kəʊtʃ] Reisebus 3.4
coal [kəʊl] Kohle E1.3
coal-mining ['kəʊlmaɪnɪŋ] Kohlenabbau, Kohlenbergbau E1.3
coastline ['kəʊstlaɪn] Küste(nlinie) E1.3
collector [kə'lektə]: **ticket collector** Fahrkartenschaffner/in, Zugbegleiter/in 3.4
come (came, come) [kʌm (keɪm, kʌm)]: **come over** vorbeikommen, herüberkommen 2.2a; **come round** *hier:* wieder zu sich kommen 10.2a; **come to mind** einfallen 4.1; **come top** an erste Stelle kommen 4.LC
comment ['kɒment] Kommentar, Bemerkung 11.3
commercial [kə'mɜːʃəl] Werbespot 2.2a
common ['kɒmən]: **have in common** gemein(sam) haben GS.4
compartment [kəm'pɑːtmənt] Abteil 3.4
compete with [kəm'piːt wɪð] antreten gegen, in Konkurrenz stehen mit 6.LC
comprehensive [ˌkɒmprɪ'hensɪv] umfassend 5.3; **comprehensive school** Gesamtschule 12.TV
compulsory [kəm'pʌlsərɪ] obligatorisch E1.1
concrete ['kɒŋkriːt] Beton 7.2a
conditions *(pl.)* [kən'dɪʃənz]: **living conditions** *(pl.)* Lebensbedingungen 7.2b
condominium *(AE)* [ˌkɒndə'mɪnɪəm] Eigentumswohnung, Wohnanlage 7.LC
confirmation [ˌkɒnfə'meɪʃən] Bestätigung 5.2a
confusing [kən'fjuːzɪŋ] verwirrend E1.2
congestion [kən'dʒestʃən] Stau 3.LC
connecting flight [kə'nektɪŋ ˌflaɪt] Anschlussflug 3.TV
consume [kən'sjuːm] konsumieren, verzehren 1.1
contents *(pl.)* ['kɒntents] Inhaltsverzeichnis 5.3
contest ['kɒntest] Wettbewerb, Wettkampf E1.2
contract ['kɒntrækt]: **fixed contract** fester Vertrag 8.TV
control [kən'trəʊl]: **be in control of** unter Kontrolle haben 3.TV
convenience [kən'viːnɪəns]: **convenience food** Fertignahrung, Fertiggerichte 5.TV; **convenience store** *(AE)* 24-Stunden-Geschäft 9.3a
conversation [ˌkɒnvə'seɪʃən]: **get into conversation** ins Gespräch kommen 1.LC
cordless ['kɔːdləs] schnurlos 8.TV
corner shop ['kɔːnə ˌʃɒp] Laden um die Ecke, Tante-Emma-Laden 9.3a
correctness [kə'rektnɪs] Genauigkeit; Korrektheit 10.LC
count [kaʊnt] zählen 7.2a
counter ['kaʊntə] *hier:* Spielmarke 12.2b
countless ['kaʊntləs] unzählig, zahllos 4.LC
cover ['kʌvə] bedecken, abdecken 4.4
craft [krɑːft] (Kunst)Handwerk E2.4
crime rate ['kraɪm ˌreɪt] Kriminalitätsrate 7.4
crisis (crises) ['kraɪsɪs ('kraɪsiːz)] Krise 11.1b
cross out [ˌkrɒs‿'aʊt] durchstreichen, ausstreichen 7.SS.1
crowd [kraʊd] (Menschen)Menge 4.4
curl up [kɜːl‿'ʌp] sich zusammenrollen 2.2a
cut off [kʌt‿'ɒf] abschneiden 2.2a
cycle path ['saɪkəl ˌpɑːθ] Radweg 3.TV

D

daffodil ['dæfədɪl] Narzisse, Osterglocke E1.1
damned [dæmd] verdammt 8.4
dance floor ['dɑːns ˌflɔː] Tanzfläche, Tanzboden 9.LC
dancing ['dɑːnsɪŋ]: **ballroom dancing** Gesellschaftstanz 6.TV; **Highland dancing** schottisches Tanzen E2.4
day out [deɪ‿'aʊt] Tagesausflug 9.LC
day-to-day [ˌdeɪtə'deɪ] (all)täglich, laufend 6.5
debit card ['debɪt ˌkɑːd] *Bankkarte mit Sofortabbuchungsfunktion (z. B. EC-Karte)* 9.3a
decide [dɪ'saɪd] (sich) entscheiden GS.5a
definitely ['defɪnɪtlɪ] definitiv, auf jeden Fall, zweifellos E2.2a
delivery service [dɪ'lɪvərɪ ˌsɜːvɪs] Lieferservice, Zustelldienst 9.TV
dental assistant [ˌdentəl‿ə'sɪstənt] Zahnarzthelfer/in 12.2a
depend on [dɪ'pend‿ɒn] abhängen von, angewiesen sein auf 10.1b
desert ['dezət] Wüste 7.2a
device [dɪ'vaɪs] Gerät 6.6
die [daɪ] sterben 7.2a
diet ['daɪət]: **be on a diet** eine Diät machen 5.2a
disabled [dɪs'eɪbəld] behindert 10.LC
disappoint [ˌdɪsə'pɔɪnt] enttäuschen 7.1
disc [dɪsk]: **floppy disc** Diskette 8.TV
dish [dɪʃ] Gericht 2.LC; **side dish** Beilage 2.LC
distance ['dɪstəns] Entfernung, Strecke E2.2a
disturb [dɪ'stɜːb] stören 2.3a
diving ['daɪvɪŋ] Tauchen 4.TV
divorce [dɪ'vɔːs] Scheidung 1.6
divorced [dɪ'vɔːst]: **get divorced** sich scheiden lassen 1.TV
do [duː]: **Will do** mach ich 1.4b; **do/get/take exercise** sich bewegen, Sport treiben 5.TV
dog [dɒg]: **take the dog for a walk** Gassi gehen 1.TV
dragon ['drægən] Drache E1.1
dreadful ['dredfəl] furchtbar, fürchterlich 4.3
dressed [drest] gekleidet E1.2
drill [drɪl] Bohrer, Bohrgerät, Bohrmaschine 8.TV
drink [drɪŋk]: **fizzy drink** Limonade 5.LC
drive off (drove, driven) [draɪv‿'ɒf (drəʊv, drɪvən)] abfahren, wegfahren 8.4
driving test ['draɪvɪŋ ˌtest] Fahrprüfung 1.4a
drop [drɒp] fallen, sinken 7.TV; **drop off** absetzen 3.LC
dryer ['draɪə]: **tumble dryer** Wäschetrockner 8.TV
duty calls ['djuːtɪ kɔːlz] die Pflicht ruft E1.2

E

earthquake ['ɜːθkweɪk] Erdbeben 7.2a
eastern ['iːstən] Ost-, östlich E2/I
easy to reach [ˌiːsɪ tə 'riːtʃ] leicht erreichbar 7.TV
economics *(pl.)* [ˌekə'nɒmɪks] Wirtschaftslehre, Wirtschaftswissenschaft(en) 12.SS.2
edge [edʒ] Rand, Kante E1.3
education [edjʊ'keɪʃən]: **adult education centre** Volkshochschule 12.TV
effect [ɪ'fekt] Auswirkung(en), Folge 1.6
elder ['eldə] älter 2.2a
electric [ɪ'lektrɪk]: **electric kettle** Wasserkocher 8.TV; **electric razor** Trockenrasierer 8.TV
electrician [ɪˌlek'trɪʃən] Elektriker/in, Elektroinstallateur/in 12.TV
elsewhere [els'weə] anderswo, sonst wo, woanders 8.3
embarrassed [ɪm'bærəst] verlegen, betreten 10.TV
emergency [ɪ'mɜːdʒənsɪ] Notfall 9.4b
encounter [ɪn'kaʊntə] Begegnung 1.LC
encounter [ɪn'kaʊntə] begegnen, in Berührung kommen mit 4.4

encourage [ɪn'kʌrɪdʒ] ermutigen 1.3

end [end]: **in the end** schlussendlich, letztendlich, schließlich 9.2

endless ['endləs] endlos, unendlich, unzählig E2.4

English-speaking ['ɪŋglɪʃ,spi:kɪŋ] englischsprachig 1.LC

enrol [ɪn'rəʊl] sich anmelden, sich einschreiben 12.SS.1

entertain [,entə'teɪn] einladen, unterhalten, bewirten 2.LC

environment-friendly [ɪn'vaɪərənmənt,frendlɪ] umweltfreundlich 3.TV

escape from [ɪ'skeɪp frəm] entrinnen, entkommen E1.3

essentially [ɪ'senʃəlɪ] hauptsächlich, im Wesentlichen, in Wirklichkeit 2.LC

estate [ɪ'steɪt]: **housing estate** Wohnanlage, (Wohn)Siedlung 7.LC

evening classes *(pl.)* ['i:vnɪŋ ,klɑ:sɪz] Abendkurse 12.TV

every now and again [,evrɪ ,naʊ_ənd_ə'gen] ab und zu, dann und wann 1.TV

exaggerate [ɪg'zædʒəreɪt] übertreiben 10.LC

exam [ɪg'zæm]: **school-leaving exam** Abschlussprüfung *(Schule)* 12.TV

example [ɪg'zɑ:mpəl]: **set an example** ein Beispiel geben 2.TV

exceptional [ɪk'sepʃənəl] außergewöhnlich, ungewöhnlich 1.6

exchange [ɪks'tʃeɪndʒ] Wortwechsel 1.4b

exciting [ɪk'saɪtɪŋ] aufregend, spannend 6.TV

excursion [ɪk'skɜ:ʃən]: **go on an excursion** einen Ausflug machen 4.TV

excuse [ɪk'skju:s] Ausrede 1.LC

exercise ['eksəsaɪz]: **do/get/take exercise** sich bewegen, Sport treiben 5.TV

exhausted [ɪg'zɔ:stɪd] erschöpft, übermüdet 3.4

exhausting [ɪg'zɔ:stɪŋ] anstrengend 4.TV

experience [ɪk'spɪərɪəns] erfahren, erleben 2.3b

extra-terrestrial [,ekstrətə'restrɪəl] Außerirdische/r 11.1a

extremely [ɪk'stri:mlɪ] äußerst, überaus 9.1

F

face to face [,feɪs tə 'feɪs] von Angesicht zu Angesicht 4.2a

fact [fækt]: **as a matter of fact** in der Tat, tatsächlich 9.1

failure ['feɪljə]: **signals failure** Signalstörung 3.4

faint [feɪnt] in Ohnmacht fallen, ohnmächtig werden 10.2a

faint [feɪnt] einer Ohnmacht nahe, schwach 10.2a

fair ['feə]: **trade fair** (Fach)Messe, Handelsmesse 1.4a

fall asleep [,fɔ:l_ə'sli:p] einschlafen 3.4

family ['fæməlɪ]: **immediate family** engste Angehörige 7.2b

far [fɑ:] *hier:* viel 4.4; **in the far north** weit oben im Norden E1.3

farewell [feə'wel] Abschied 12.ST

farmer ['fɑ:mə] Bauer/Bäuerin 10.SS.1

farming ['fɑ:mɪŋ] Agrar-, Landwirtschafts- E2.4

fashion ['fæʃən] Mode 11.1a

fatty ['fætɪ] fettig, fetthaltig 5.1

fault [fɔ:lt] Schuld, Verschulden 2.SST

faulty ['fɔ:ltɪ] defekt, fehlerhaft 8.4

fear [fɪə] Angst, Furcht 5.LC

feel sick [fi:l 'sɪk] sich schlecht fühlen 2.3a

fever ['fi:və] Fieber 11.1a

file [faɪl] Datei 8.4; **back up file** Sicherungskopie 8.4

fill up [,fɪl_'ʌp] (auf)füllen 4.4

filler ['fɪlə] Flickwort, Füllwort 6.3

filthy ['fɪlθɪ] dreckig, schmutzig 4.TV

fine art [faɪn_'ɑ:t] schöne Künste E2.4

first aid [,fɜ:st_'eɪd] erste Hilfe 12.1

fit [fɪt] Anfall 1.LC

fixed contract [fɪkst 'kɒntrækt] fester Vertrag 8.TV

fizzy drink ['fɪzɪ ,drɪŋk] Limonade 5.LC

flight [flaɪt]: **connecting flight** Anschlussflug 3.TV; **flight attendant** Flugbegleiter/in 10.LC

flood [flʌd] Flut, Hochwasser, Überschwemmung 7.TV

flood [flʌd] (über)fluten, überschwemmen 8.4

floodlit ['flʌdlɪt] (mit Flutlicht) angestrahlt 7.2a

floor [flɔ:]: **dance floor** Tanzfläche, Tanzboden 9.LC

floppy disc [,flɒpɪ 'dɪsk] Diskette 8.TV

fly by [,flaɪ 'baɪ] wie im Flug vergehen 12.2a

foggy ['fɒgɪ] neblig 7.TV

food [fu:d] *hier:* Nahrungsmittel 5.1; **convenience food** Fertignahrung, Fertiggerichte 5.TV

for a while [,fər_ə 'waɪl] eine Zeit lang 1.6

form [fɔ:m] formen, bilden, entstehen E1.K

fortress ['fɔ:trəs] Festung E1.3

fortunately ['fɔ:tʃənətlɪ] glücklicherweise 10.SS.T

frequently ['fri:kwəntlɪ] oft, häufig 1.1

friend [frend]: **close friend** enge/r Freund/in 2.1

frightened ['fraɪtnd]: **be frightened of** Angst haben vor 10.1a

frightening ['fraɪtnɪŋ] beängstigend, erschreckend 10.2c

full [fʊl] *hier:* satt 4.4

fun [fʌn]: **have fun** Spaß haben 9.1

further ['fɜ:ðə] weitere(r, s); weiter 4.2b

G

gadget ['gædʒɪt] Gerät, Apparat 8.2

games *(pl.)* [geɪmz]: **board games** *(pl.)* Brettspiele 6.TV

gang [gæŋ] Bande 7.2a

gap [gæp] Lücke, Kluft, Spalt 10.4

garage sale ['gærɑ:ʒ ,seɪl] *privater Flohmarkt in der Garage* 9.3a

gardening tool ['gɑ:dənɪŋ ,tu:l] Gartengerät 9.3a

general knowledge [,dʒenərəl 'nɒlɪdʒ] Allgemeinbildung 6.LC

gentle ['dʒentl] mild E2.4

gently ['dʒentlɪ] sanft E2.4

germ [dʒɜ:m] (Krankheits)Keim 10.1a

get (got, got) [get (gɒt, gɒt)]: **get a lift** (im Auto) mitgenommen werden 10.SS.2; **get promotion** befördert werden 1.TV; **get a suntan** braun werden 4.TV; **get away from** wegkommen von, entkommen, entfliehen 7.LC; **get back from/to** zurückkommen aus/nach 1.4a; **get bored** sich langweilen 12.SS.3; **get divorced** sich scheiden lassen 1.TV; **get good value for money** etw. für sein Geld bekommen 9.SS.3; **get into (got, got)** einsteigen 10.2a; **get into conversation** ins Gespräch kommen 1.LC; **get lost** *hier:* sich vertiefen 6.5; **get on with** klarkommen mit, auskommen mit 2.2a; **get one's tongue around** etwas nicht aussprechen können, sich die Zunge fast abbrechen E1.2; **get rid of** loswerden, sich befreien von 5.3; **get started** beginnen GS.I; **get stuck in** festsitzen 5.4; **get used to** sich gewöhnen an 4.4; **do/ get/take exercise** sich bewegen, Sport treiben 5.TV

give someone a ring [,gɪv sʌmwʌn_ə 'rɪŋ] jdn. anrufen 1.4b

glitter ['glɪtə] funkeln, glänzen, gleißen, glitzern E2.4

go [gəʊ]: **go down** fallen 5.2b; **go on an excursion** einen Ausflug machen 4.TV; **go to the seaside** ans Meer fahren 4.TV; **go together** zusammenpassen 3.SS.2

good-looking [,gʊd'lʊkɪŋ] gut aussehend 11.TV

grade [greɪd] Note 12.TV

grammar school ['græmə ,sku:l] Gymnasium 12.TV

grandfather ['grænd,fɑ:ðə] Großvater 11.4

grandson ['grænsʌn] Enkel(sohn) 1.4a
greet [gri:t] grüßen 1.5
groceries *(pl.)* ['grəʊsərɪz] Lebensmittel 9.3a
ground [graʊnd]: **breeding ground** Brutstätte, Brutplatz E1.3
grow into ['grəʊ‿ˌɪntə] werden zu 5.LC
guard [gɑ:d]: **security guard** Sicherheitspersonal 9.LC
guess [ges]: **I guess you're right.** Du hast wohl Recht. 4.4
guide [gaɪd] Leitfaden, Führer 5.3
guilty ['gɪltɪ] schuldig 6.5
gum [gʌm]: **chewing gum** Kaugummi 5.5

H

habit ['hæbɪt]: **viewing habit** Fernsehgewohnheit 1.1
haggle over ['hægl‿ˌəʊvə] feilschen über 4.4
hairy ['heərɪ] haarig, behaart 7.2a
handicapped ['hændɪkæpt] behindert 10.LC
handicrafts *(pl.)* ['hændɪˌkrɑ:fts] Bastelarbeit 6.2
handle ['hændl] (Hand)Griff 8.2
handwriting ['hændˌraɪtɪŋ] Handschrift 12.2a
hang up [hæŋ‿'ʌp] aufhängen 8.2
have [hæv]: **have a blank** *(informal)* einen Blackout haben 10.2a; **have butterflies in one's stomach** das Flattern haben 10.2a; **have fun** Spaß haben 9.1; **have in common** gemein(sam) haben GS.4
head back [ˌhed 'bæk] zurückgehen 7.LC
health [helθ]: **be in good/poor health** in/bei guter/schlechter Gesundheit sein 5.TV; **health-conscious** gesundheitsbewusst 5.TV
heart [hɑ:t]: **at heart** im Grunde (seines Herzens) E2.4
heat [hi:t] Hitze 4.4
heat [hi:t] erwärmen, erhitzen, heizen 8.2
hello [hə'ləʊ]: **say hello to** grüßen 1.4b
herbal ['hɜ:bəl] Kräuter- 5.5
heritage ['herɪtɪdʒ] Erbe, Erbschaft E1.3
hidden ['hɪdən] versteckt 5.3
hide and seek [ˌhaɪd‿ənd 'si:k] Verstecken, Versteckspiel 11.TV
high-heeled [ˌhaɪ'hi:ld] mit hohen Absätzen 11.TV
Highland dancing ['haɪlænd ˌdɑ:nsɪŋ] schottisches Tanzen E2.4
hike [haɪk] wandern E2.4
hill [hɪl] Hügel 6.5
history ['hɪstərɪ] Geschichte E1.3
hit (hit, hit) [hɪt (hɪt, hɪt)] treffen, schlagen 5.4
hold onto (held, held) [ˌhəʊld‿'ɒntu: (held, held)] festhalten an 10.SS.1
hole [həʊl] Loch 8.SS.1
holy ['həʊlɪ]: **holy water** Weihwasser 4.4
home [həʊm]: **nursing home** Pflegeheim 7.3a
hoover ['hu:və] staubsaugen 1.SS.3
horrible ['hɒrɪbl] schrecklich, fürchterlich 3.4
hospitable ['hɒspɪtəbəl] gastfreundlich 4.4
host [həʊst] Gastgeber 2.LC
hostel ['hɒstl]: **youth hostel** Jugendherberge 4.1
hostess ['həʊstəs]: **air hostess** Stewardess 10.LC
house [haʊs]: **move house** umziehen 1.TV
household task [ˌhaʊshəʊld 'tɑ:sk] Aufgabe/Arbeit im Haushalt 6.2
housing ['haʊzɪŋ] Unterkunft 7.4; **housing estate** Wohnanlage, (Wohn)Siedlung 7.LC
how's it going? [ˌhaʊs‿ɪt 'gəʊɪŋ] wie geht's? GS.5a
humid ['hju:mɪd] feucht 7.TV
hunter ['hʌntə] Jäger/in E2.3
hurricane ['hʌrɪkən] Hurrikan, Orkan, Wirbelsturm 7.TV

I

illness ['ɪlnɪs] Krankheit 1.6
image ['ɪmɪdʒ] Bild(nis) E1.3
immediate family [ɪ'mi:dɪət ˌfæməlɪ] engste Angehörige 7.2b
immigrant ['ɪmɪgrənt] Einwanderer, Zuwanderer E2.2a
impolite [ˌɪmpə'laɪt] unhöflich GS.5a
impressed [ɪm'prest] beeindruckt GS.5a
impulse ['ɪmpʌls]: **on impulse** impulsiv, spontan 9.1
in the far north [ˌɪn ðə ˌfɑ: 'nɔ:θ] weit oben im Norden E1.3
in-built ['ɪnbɪlt] eingebaut 8.LC
in-service training [ɪn'sɜ:vɪs ˌtreɪnɪŋ] Ausbildung am Arbeitsplatz, berufsbegleitende Ausbildung 12.TV
incredible [ɪn'kredɪbəl] unglaublich 9.LC
indoor ['ɪndɔ:] im Haus, innen 6.2
industrial area [ɪnˌdʌstrɪəl‿'eərɪə] Industriegebiet, Gewerbegebiet 7.TV
inexpensive [ˌɪnɪks'pensɪv] kostengünstig, preiswert 7.4
inexperienced [ˌɪnɪk'spɪərɪənst] unerfahren, unbewandert 11.TV
inherit [ɪn'herɪt] erben 9.TV
insecurity [ˌɪnsɪ'kjʊərətɪ] Ungewissheit, Unsicherheit 5.4
insomnia [ɪn'sɒmnɪə] Schlaflosigkeit 5.3
instructor [ɪn'strʌktə] Ausbilder/in, Lehrer/in 10.2a
interrupt [ˌɪntə'rʌpt] unterbrechen, *hier:* stören 8.LC
introduction [ˌɪntrə'dʌkʃən] Einführung 11.1b
Inuit *(pl.)* ['ɪnjuɪt] Inuit, Eskimos E2.3
invest [ɪn'vest] investieren, anlegen 9.TV
ironworks *(pl.)* ['aɪnwɜ:ks] Eisenwerk, Eisenhütte E1.3
Iroquois ['ɪrəkwɔɪ] Irokese/Irokesin E2.3
isolated ['aɪsəleɪtɪd] abgelegen 7.TV
issue ['ɪʃu:] *hier.* Frage, Problem 5.3

J

jacket ['dʒækɪt]: **life jacket** Schwimmweste 6.4b
Jeweller`s ['dʒʊələz] Juwelier 9.TV
jewellery ['dʒu:əlrɪ] Schmuck 9.4a
join in ['dʒɔn‿ɪn] mitmachen, sich beteiligen 4.4
joke [dʒəʊk] Witz 10.2a
juggle ['dʒʌgəl] jonglieren 12.1
jump [dʒʌmp] Sprung 10.2b
jungle ['dʒʌŋgəl] Dschungel 7.2a

K

keep [ki:p]: **keep a record of s.th.** etw. schriftlich festhalten, Aufzeichnungen von etw. machen 9.1; **keep doing** weiterhin tun GS.5a
kettle ['ketl]: **electric kettle** Wasserkocher 8.TV
keyboard ['ki:bɔ:d] Tastatur 8.TV
knee-length ['ni:ˌleŋθ] knielang 11.SS.3
knowledge ['nɒlɪdʒ]: **general knowledge** Allgemeinbildung 6.LC

L

labour-saving ['leɪbəˌseɪvɪŋ] arbeitssparend 6.6
lake [leɪk] See 9.LC
last but not least [ˌlɑ:st bət nɒt 'li:st] nicht zuletzt E1.3
laugh [lɑ:f] lachen 10.2a
law [lɔ:] Gesetz E1.2
lawn [lɔ:n] Rasen 1.TV
lawnmower ['lɔ:nˌməʊə] Rasenmäher 8.TV

leaflet ['liːflət] Prospekt 9.4b
least ['liːst]: **last but not least** nicht zuletzt E1.3
leisure time ['leʒə taɪm] Freizeit 6.LC
level ['levəl] Pegel, Level, Niveau 7.4
lie (lay, lain) [laɪ (leɪ, leɪn)] liegen 4.TV
life jacket ['laɪf ˌdʒækɪt] Schwimmweste 6.4b
lift [lɪft]: **get a lift** (im Auto) mitgenommen werden 10.SS.2
lighthouse ['laɪthaʊs] Leuchtturm E2.4
like [laɪk]: **things like that** so was 2.2a
limit ['lɪmɪt]: **speed limit** Geschwindigkeitsbegrenzung 3.TV
line [laɪn]: **railway line** Eisenbahnlinie, Bahnstrecke E1.3
list [lɪst]: **shopping list** Einkaufsliste, Einkaufszettel 9.4b
litter ['lɪtə] Abfall 9.LC
living conditions *(pl.)* ['lɪvɪŋ kənˌdɪʃənz] Lebensbedingungen 7.2b
loan [ləʊn]: **bank loan** Bankdarlehen, Bankkredit 9.1
lobster ['lɒbstə] Hummer E2.4
local call ['ləʊkəl ˌkɔːl] Ortsgespräch 8.TV
lonely ['ləʊnlɪ] einsam 11.TV
loner ['ləʊnə] Einzelgänger/in 2.TV
long-distance call [lɒŋ'dɪstəns ˌkɔːl] Ferngespräch 8.TV
long-term [ˌlɒŋ'tɜːm] Langzeit- 1.6
longer ['lɒŋə]: **no longer** nicht mehr 5.LC
look [lʊk] aussehen 9.1; **look up** nachschlagen GS.5a
lord [lɔːd] Herr 11.1a
lose [luːz]: **lose touch with** Kontakt verlieren mit 2.TV; **lose weight** abnehmen 5.2a
lost [lɒst]: **get lost** *hier:* sich vertiefen 6.5
lottery ticket ['lɒtərɪ ˌtɪkɪt] Lotterielos 9.4b
lounge bar ['laʊndʒ bɑː] *der vornehmere Teil eines Pubs mit eigener Bar* 6.LC
low [ləʊ] gering, niedrig 5.5; **low-fat** fettarm, fettreduziert 5.TV; **low-heeled** mit niedrigen Absätzen 11.TV
lucky you [ˌlʌkɪ 'juː] hast du ein Glück! 1.4a

M

machine [mə'ʃiːn]: **telephone answering machine** Anrufbeantworter 8.TV
magic ['mædʒɪk] Zauber- 12.1
magnificent [mæg'nɪfɪsənt] großartig, herrlich 4.TV
main street ['meɪn striːt] Hauptstraße 9.4a
maintenance ['meɪntənəns] Instandhaltung, Wartung 12.3a
major road [ˌmeɪdʒə 'rəʊd] Hauptverkehrsstraße 7.TV
make a mess [ˌmeɪk_ə 'mes] Unordnung machen 1.1
make oneself understood [ˌmeɪk wʌnˌself_ʌndə'stʊd] sich verständlich machen 2.3a
make s.o welcome [ˌmeɪk sʌmwʌn 'welkəm] jdn. sehr freundlich aufnehmen 4.4
manager ['mænɪdʒə]: **sales manager** Verkaufsleiter/in, Vertriebsleiter/in 12.TV
manual ['mænjʊəl] manuell; *hier:* mechanisch 8.TV
maple ['meɪpəl] Ahorn E2.4
marbles ['mɑːbəlz] Murmeln 11.TV
mark [mɑːk] Zensur, Schulnote 12.2a
marvellous ['mɑːvələs] fabelhaft, fantastisch, großartig 4.3
master ['mɑːstə] Meister 12.TV
maths *(pl.)* [mæθs] Mathematik 12.2a
matter ['mætər]: **as a matter of fact** in der Tat, tatsächlich 9.1
medieval [ˌmedɪ'iːvəl] mittelalterlich E1.3
memo ['meməʊ] Notiz(zettel), Kurzmitteilung 8.TV
mess [mes]: **make a mess** in Unordnung bringen 1.1
middle ['mɪdl]: **middle name** zweiter Vorname GS.1; **in the middle of nowhere** am Ende der Welt 3.4; **middle-aged** mittleren Alters 11.TV
mind [maɪnd]: **come to mind** einfallen 4.1; **My mind went blank.** *(informal)* Ich hatte einen Blackout. GS.5a
mind [maɪnd]: **I don't mind.** Ich habe nichts dagegen. 3.4; **mind you** wohlgemerkt 2.2a
miss a turn [ˌmɪs_ə 'tɜːn] eine Runde aussetzen 12.2b
missing ['mɪsɪŋ] fehlend 1.4b
mistake [mɪ'steɪk] Fehler, Irrtum 4.4
misunderstanding [ˌmɪsʌndə'stændɪŋ] Missverständnis 2.3b
mix [mɪks] Mischung E2.4
modern-day ['mɒdndeɪ] heutig, von heute 5.4
money ['mʌnɪ]: **get good value for money** etw. für sein Geld bekommen 9.SS.3
moorland ['mʊələnd] Heideland, Heidemoor E1.3
moose (moose) [muːs] Elch E2.4
morning ['mɔːnɪŋ]: **in the early mornings** frühmorgens 1.TV
mother tongue ['mʌðə ˌtʌŋ] Muttersprache E2.3
move [muːv] *hier:* (sich) bewegen 4.4; **move house** umziehen 1.TV
mow [məʊ] mähen 1.TV
mudbath ['mʌdbɑːθ] Moorbad, Schlammbad 5.3
mudslide ['mʌdslaɪd] Murenabgang 7.2a
musician [mjuː'zɪʃən] Musiker/in E1.2

N

name [neɪm]: **middle name** zweiter Vorname GS.1
name after [neɪm_'ɑːftə] benennen nach E1.3
narrow ['nærəʊ] eng, schmal 7.TV
native speaker [ˌneɪtɪv 'spiːkə] Muttersprachler/in 3.SST
neighborhood *(AE)* ['neɪbəhʊd] Nachbarschaft 7.2a
neighbourhood ['neɪbəhʊd] Nachbarschaft 2.4
newly ['njuːlɪ] neu(lich) 9.SS.3
nickname ['nɪkneɪm] Spitzname GS.1
nightlife ['naɪtlaɪf] Nachtleben 7.3b
no longer [nəʊ 'lɒŋə] nicht mehr 5.LC
northernmost ['nɔːðənməʊst] nördlichst 7.2a
now [naʊ]: **every now and again** ab und zu, dann und wann 1.TV
nowhere ['nəʊweə]: **in the middle of nowhere** am Ende der Welt 3.4
number ['nʌmbə] (durch)nummerieren GS.2
numerous ['njuːmərəs] zahlreich E1.3
nursery school ['nɜːsərɪ ˌskuːl] Kindergarten; Vorschule 7.3a
nursing home ['nɜːsɪŋ ˌhəʊm] Pflegeheim 7.3a

O

obese [əʊ'biːs] mollig, korpulent, fettleibig 5.LC
occupation [ˌɒkjʊ'peɪʃən] Beschäftigung, Tätigkeit 6.1
odd [ɒd] merkwürdig, sonderbar 11.SS.3
off [ˌtaɪm_'ɒf]: **time off** Freizeit 2.2a
offend [ə'fend] angreifen, beleidigen, verletzen 10.LC
OK [əʊ'keɪ]: **That's OK with me.** Das ist in Ordnung für mich. 2.2a
old-age pensioner [əʊldˌeɪdʒ 'penʃənə] Pensionär/in, Rentner/in 2.TV
on average [ɒn_'ævərɪdʒ] im Durchschnitt 1.1
on impulse [ɒn_'ɪmpʌls] impulsiv, spontan 9.1
on one's own [ˌɒn wʌnz_'əʊn] allein 2.2a
one-third [ˌwʌn'θɜːd] ein Drittel 5.LC
open space [ˌəʊpən 'speɪs] Freifläche 7.4
opinion poll [ə'pɪnjən ˌpəʊl] Meinungsumfrage 1.1
ordinary ['ɔːdənərɪ]: **out of the ordinary** ungewöhnlich 1.6

origin ['ɒrɪdʒɪn] Herkunft, Ursprung 4.LC
out of the ordinary [ˌaʊt‿əv ðɪ‿'ɔːdənərɪ] ungewöhnlich 1.6
outdoor ['aʊtdɔː] draußen, im Freien 6.2
outskirts *(pl.)* ['aʊtskɜːts] Stadtrand(gebiet), Vorort 7.TV
over ['əʊvə] *hier:* vorbei 1.4a
overcome [ˌəʊvə'kʌm] bewältigen, überwinden 2.TV
overnight ['əʊvənaɪt] über Nacht 1.6
overwork [ˌəʊvə'wɜːk] (Arbeits)Überlastung 5.4
own [əʊn]: **on one's own** allein 2.2a

P

pace [peɪs] Geschwindigkeit, Tempo E2.4
package tour ['pækɪdʒ ˌtʊə] Pauschalreise, Pauschalurlaub 4.TV
pain [peɪn] Schmerz 5.3
parachute ['pærəʃuːt] Fallschirm 10.2b
Parisian [pə'rɪzɪən] pariserisch E2.4
parking ticket ['pɑːkɪŋ ˌtɪkɪt] Strafzettel 3.2b
part [pɑːt]: **take part** teilnehmen 10.3; **play a part** eine Rolle spielen 1.3
particular [pə'tɪkjʊlə] besondere(r, s), speziell 1.4b
pasture ['pɑːstʃə] Weide(land), Gras E2.4
path [pɑːθ]: **cycle path** Radweg 3.TV
patience ['peɪʃənts] Geduld 6.TV
patron saint ['peɪtrən ˌseɪnt] Schutzpatron, Schutzheilige/r E1.3
pause [pɔːz]: **pause button** Pausentaste 5.SS.2b
pay [peɪ]: **pay attention to** Aufmerksamkeit schenken, beachten 1.4b; **pay cash** bar zahlen 9.1; **pay for** (be)zahlen für 4.4
peace [piːs] Friede(n), Ruhe E2.4
peaceful ['piːsfəl] friedlich, ruhig 6.4b
pensioner ['penʃənə]: **old-age pensioner** Pensionär/in, Rentner/in 2.TV
percentage [pə'sentɪdʒ] Prozentanteil, Prozentsatz 5.LC
perm [pɜːm] Dauerwelle 11.TV
personal space [ˌpɜːsənəl 'speɪs] persönlicher Freiraum 4.4
pharmacy *(AE)* ['fɑːməsɪ] Apotheke 9.3a
phone [fəʊn]: **cell phone** Mobiltelefon, Handy 8.SS.2
phone-in ['fəʊnɪn] *Sendung mit telefonischer Publikumsbeteiligung* 2.2a
physically ['fɪzɪklɪ] physisch; körperlich 10.LC
physics *(pl.)* ['fɪzɪks] Physik 12.TV
picturesque [ˌpɪktʃə'resk] malerisch, pittoresk 4.TV
pit [pɪt] Bergwerk, Schacht(anlage) E1.3
plait [plæt] Zopf 11.TV
plate [pleɪt] Teller 4.4
platform shoe [ˌplætfɔːm 'ʃuː] Plateauschuh 11.1a
play [pleɪ] Spiel, *hier:* Theaterstück 11.3
play [pleɪ]: **play a part** eine Rolle spielen 1.3; **play tag** Fangen spielen 11.TV
playgroup ['pleɪgruːp] Spielgruppe, Krabbelgruppe; Kindergarten 12.TV
pleasant ['plezənt] angenehm, freundlich 1.LC
pleasantly ['plezəntlɪ] angenehm 7.1
pleasure ['pleʃə] Freude, Genuss, Vergnügen 6.5
plumber ['plʌmə] Installateur/in 12.TV
poll [pəʊl]: **opinion poll** Meinungsumfrage 1.1
polluted [pə'luːtɪd] (umwelt)verschmutzt 7.TV
ponytail ['pəʊnɪteɪl] Pferdeschwanz 11.SS.3
portable ['pɔːtəbəl] tragbar 8.TV
potluck [ˌpɒt'lʌk] *Essen, bei dem jeder Gast eine Speise mitbringt* 2.LC
pouring ['pɔːrɪŋ] strömend 9.LC
powerless ['paʊələs] kraftlos, machtlos 5.4
pre-Christmas sale [priː'krɪstməs‿seɪl] Vorweihnachtsgeschäft 9.3a
pregnant ['pregnənt] schwanger 1.4a
present day [ˌprezənt 'deɪ]: **to the present day** bis zum heutigen Tag E1.K
press [pres] drücken 1.1
pressure ['preʃə]: **under time pressure** unter Zeitdruck 5.4
pretty ['prɪtɪ] *hier:* ziemlich E1.2
printer ['prɪntə] Drucker 8.TV
progress ['prəʊgrəs]: **in progress** im Gange, im Werden 3.4
promotion [prə'məʊʃən] Beförderung 1.TV; **get promotion** befördert werden 1.TV
proper ['prɒpə] richtig, echt E2.2a
proposed [prə'pəʊzd] geplant E1.2
proud of ['praʊd‿əv] stolz auf GS.5a
prune [pruːn] beschneiden 12.1
pub-crawl ['pʌbkrɔːl] Kneipentour 6.LC
public ['pʌblɪk] : **public bar** Ausschank, Schänke 6.LC; **public school** Privatschule E1.K
pull-out ['pulaʊt] heraustrennbar 5.3
pupil ['pjuːpəl] Schüler/in 12.LC
purpose ['pɜːpəs] Zweck, Ziel 3.1
purse [pɜːs] Geldbeutel, Geldbörse6.3
put on weight [ˌpʊt‿ɒn 'weɪt] zunehmen, Gewicht ansetzen 5.TV

Q

question tag ['kwestʃən ˌtæg] Frageanhängsel 5.2a
quiet ['kwaɪət] Ruhe E2.4

R

radio-controlled ['reɪdɪəʊkən'trəʊld] funkgesteuert 9.LC
railway line ['reɪlweɪ ˌlaɪn] Eisenbahnlinie, Bahnstrecke E1.3
raise [reɪs] aufbringen, beschaffen 2.4
rate [reɪt]: **crime rate** Kriminalitätsrate 7.4
Rather you than me. [ˌrɑːðə ˌjʊ ðən 'miː] Das würde ich bestimmt nicht machen wollen. 4.2a
raw [rɔː] roh E2.3
razor ['reɪzə]: **electric razor** Trockenrasierer 8.TV
re-enact [ˌriːɪ'nækt] nachstellen E2.4
reach [riːtʃ]: **easy to reach** leicht erreichbar 7.TV
react [rɪ'ækt] reagieren 1.4a
realise ['rɪəlaɪz] verwirklichen, durchführen, in die Praxis umsetzen 7.LC
rearrange [ˌriːə'reɪndʒ] neu (an)ordnen 12.SS.1
reasonable ['riːsənəbl] vernünftig 9.SS.3
rebellious [rɪ'beljəs] aufsässig, rebellisch 11.TV
recipe ['resɪpɪ] Rezept 5.5
record ['rekəd]: **keep a record of s.th.** etw. schriftlich festhalten, Aufzeichnungen von etw. machen 9.1
regularly ['regjʊləlɪ] regelmäßig 2.2a
related to [rɪ'leɪtɪd tə] verwandt mit E1.2
relaxation [ˌriːlæk'seɪʃən] Entspannung 4.1
relaxed [rɪ'lækst] entspannt 1.4a
relaxing [rɪ'læksɪŋ] entspannend 4.3
rely on [rɪ'laɪ‿ɒn] sich verlassen auf 2.2a
remainder [rɪ'meɪndə]: **the remainder** der Rest, die Übrigen 12.LC
remark [rɪ'mɑːk] Bemerkung 4.2a
remedy ['remɪdɪ] Gegenmittel 5.3
reread (reread, reread) [rɪ'riːd (rɪ'red, rɪ'red)] nochmals lesen, wieder lesen 6.5
residential area [resɪ'denʃəl‿'eərɪə] Wohngebiet, Wohngegend 7.TV
responsible [rɪ'spɒnsɪbəl] verantwortlich 11.5

retell [ˌriːˈtel] nacherzählen; nochmals erzählen; weitererzählen 10.2b
retirement [rɪˈtaɪəmənt] Ruhestand, Pensionierung 7.LC
retrain [ˌriːˈtreɪn] umschulen 12.2a
revolving [rɪˈvɒlvɪŋ] sich drehend 9.LC
rid [rɪd]: **get rid of** loswerden, sich befreien von 5.3
ring [rɪŋ]: **give someone a ring** jdn. anrufen 1.4b
rise [raɪs]: **on the rise** im Zunehmen 8.LC
risk [rɪsk]: **take a risk** ein Risiko eingehen 9.1
road [rəʊd]: **major road** Hauptverkehrsstraße 7.TV; **road sign** Straßenschild E1.2
rolling [ˈrəʊlɪŋ] sanft geschwungen E2.4
rowing [ˈrəʊɪŋ] Ruder- 5.5
rubber [ˈrʌbə] (Radier)Gummi 12.2b
rural [ˈruərəl] ländlich, bäuerlich 7.TV

S

sail [seɪl] segeln 12.2a
sailing [ˈseɪlɪŋ] Segeln, Segelsport 4.TV
saint [seɪnt]: **patron saint** Schutzpatron, Schutzheilige/r E1.3
sale [seɪl]: **garage sale** *privater Flohmarkt in der Garage* 9.3a; **pre-Christmas sale** Vorweihnachtsgeschäft 9.3a; **summer sale** Sommerschlussverkauf 9.3a
sales manager [ˈseɪlz ˌmænɪdʒə] Verkaufsleiter/in, Vertriebsleiter/in 12.TV
salt [sɔːlt]: **bath salts** Badesalz 6.5
say hello to [ˌseɪ həˈləʊ tə] grüßen 1.4b
scared [skeəd] erschrocken, verängstigt 10.1b
scarf (scarfs/scarves) [skɑːf (skɑːvz)] Schal 11.TV
scary [ˈskeərɪ] Furcht erregend, schaurig 10.1b
scenery [ˈsiːnərɪ] Landschaft 4.TV
school [skuːl]: **boarding school** Internat 12.TV; **comprehensive school** Gesamtschule 12.TV; **grammar school** Gymnasium 12.TV; **nursery school** Kindergarten; Vorschule 7.3a; **public school** Privatschule E1.K; **secondary school** weiterführende Schule, höhere Schule 12.TV; **single sex school** Jungen- *bzw.* Mädchenschule 12.TV; **school-leaving exam** Abschlussprüfung *(Schule)* 12.TV
science [ˈsaɪəns] (Natur)Wissenschaft 12.TV
scooter [ˈskuːtə] Roller 11.TV
Scot [skɒt] Schotte/Schottin E2.4
scream [skriːm] schreien 5.4
screen [skriːn] Bildschirm, Monitor 5.4
seal [siːl] Seehund, Robbe E1.3
seasick [ˈsiːsɪk] seekrank 3.TV
seaside [ˈsiːsaɪd]: **go to the seaside** ans Meer fahren 4.TV
secondary school [ˈsekəndərɪ ˌskuːl] weiterführende Schule, höhere Schule 12.TV
section [ˈsekʃən] Teil, Abschnitt 5.3
security guard [sɪˈkjʊərətɪ ˌɡɑːd] Sicherheitspersonal 9.LC
seek [siːk]: **hide and seek** Verstecken, Versteckspiel 11.TV
seldom [ˈseldəm] selten, rar 2.SS.4
self [self]: **self-catering accommodation** Unterkunft für Selbstversorger 4.TV; **self-confident** selbstbewusst 11.5; **self-conscious** befangen, gehemmt 10.SS.3
senior citizen [ˈsiːnɪə ˌsɪtɪzən] Senior/in 2.TV
seriously [ˈsɪrɪəslɪ] ernst(haft), schwer 5.SS.3
service [ˈsɜːvɪs]: **delivery service** Lieferservice, Zustelldienst 9.TV
set [set (set, set)] Satz 6.3
set an example [ˌset‿ən‿ɪɡˈzɑːmpəl] ein Beispiel geben 2.TV
settle [ˈsetl] (sich) ansiedeln, (sich) niederlassen E2.2a
sex [seks]: **single sex school** Jungen- *bzw.* Mädchenschule 12.TV
shake [ʃeɪk] zittern 10.2a
shape [ʃeɪp]: **be in good/bad shape** in guter/schlechter Verfassung sein 5.TV
share [ʃeə] Aktie 9.1
sheep *(sheep)* [ʃiːp (ʃiːp)] Schaf E1.1
sheltered [ˈʃeltəd] geschützt E1.3
shirt [ʃɜːt] Hemd 11.TV
shoe [ʃuː]: **platform shoe** Plateauschuh 11.1a
shop [ʃɒp]: **corner shop** Laden um die Ecke, Tante-Emma-Laden 9.3a
shopper [ˈʃɒpə] Käufer/in 9.LC
shopping [ˈʃɒpɪŋ]: **shopping centre** Einkaufszentrum 9.3a; **shopping channel** Einkaufsfernsehen 9.3a; **shopping list** Einkaufsliste, Einkaufszettel 9.4b; **shopping trolley** Einkaufswagen 9.1
short of breath [ˌʃɔːt‿əv ˈbreθ] außer Atem, kurzatmig 5.TV
shorten [ˈʃɔːtn] kürzen GS.1
shoulder-length [ˈʃəʊldə ˌleŋθ] schulterlang 11.TV
shower [ˈʃaʊə]: **bridal shower** *Brautparty, bei der Geschenke überreicht werden* 2.LC
shy [ʃaɪ] schüchtern 11.5
sick [sɪk]: **feel sick** sich schlecht fühlen 2.3a
side dish [ˈsaɪd‿dɪʃ] Beilage 2.LC
sign [saɪn]: **road sign** Straßenschild E1.2
signal [ˈsɪɡnəl] signalisieren 1.SST
signals failure [ˈsɪɡnəlz ˌfeɪljə] Signalstörung 3.4
silence [ˈsaɪləns] Stille, Ruhe; Schweigen 4.4
silly [ˈsɪlɪ] albern, dumm GS.5a
simply [ˈsɪmplɪ] einfach, nur 10.LC
single [ˈsɪŋɡəl] *hier:* alleinerziehend 2.2a; **single sex school** Jungen- *bzw.* Mädchenschule 12.TV
skate [skeɪt] Schlittschuh E2.2a
ski trail [ˈskiː treɪl] Skipiste, Loipe 7.2a
skip [skɪp] *hier:* seilspringen 11.TV
skirt [skɜːt] Rock 4.4
skittles *(pl.)* [ˈskɪtlz] Kegel(spiel) 6.TV
sleepy [ˈsliːpɪ] verschlafen E2.4
sleeveless [ˈsliːvləs] ärmellos 4.4
smash [smæʃ] zerschlagen, zerschmettern 8.4
snack [snæk] Imbiss 5.LC
snooze button [ˈsnuːz ˌbʌtn] Schlummertaste 1.1
snow-shoe [ˈsnəʊʃuː] mit Schneeschuhen gehen E2.4
snowy [ˈsnəʊɪ] verschneit E2.4
so-called [ˌsəʊˈkɔːld] so genannte(r, s) 3.LC
soak in the bath [ˌsəʊk‿ɪn ðə ˈbɑːθ] lange in der Wanne liegen 6.5
solution [səˈluːʃən] Lösung 5.3
someday [ˈsʌmdeɪ] eines Tages, irgendeinmal 10.3
sometime [ˈsʌmtaɪm] irgendwann 1.4b
soon [suːn]: **as soon as** sobald 1.1
soup [suːp] Suppe 4.4
southern [ˈsʌðən] Süd-, südlich E2.3
space [speɪs]: **open space** Freifläche 7.4; **personal space** persönlicher Freiraum 4.4
speaker [ˈspiːkə]: **native speaker** Muttersprachler/in 3.SST
speech [spiːtʃ] Rede 10.2a
speed limit [ˈspiːd ˌlɪmɪt] Geschwindigkeitsbegrenzung 3.TV
spider [ˈspaɪdə] Spinne 7.2a
spill (spilt, spilt) [spɪl (spɪlt, spɪlt)] verschütten 8.4
spoilt [spɔɪlt]: **be spoilt for choice** die Qual der Wahl haben 4.LC
spree [spriː] Orgie 9.1
stair [steə] Stufe, Treppe 5.1
stamina [ˈstæmɪnə] Ausdauer, Durchhaltevermögen 6.TV
stammer [ˈstæmə] stammeln, stottern 10.2a
started [ˈstɑːtɪd]: **get started** beginnen GS.I
state [steɪt] nennen, angeben 3.1
stay tuned [steɪ ˈtjuːnd] dran bleiben 2.2a
steam [stiːm] Dampf 8.TV
steep [stiːp] steil E1.3
stomach [ˈstʌmək]: **have butterflies in one's stomach** das Flattern haben 10.2a

store ['stɔː]: **convenience store** *(AE)* 24-Stunden-Geschäft 9.3a; **store credit card** Kundenkarte 9.3a
storm [stɔːm] Gewitter, Sturm 10.SS.2
street [striːt]: **main street** Hauptstraße 9.4a
strength [streŋθ] Stärke, Kraft 6.TV
strengthen ['streŋθən] stärken, festigen E1.3
stress [stres] betonen 10.SS.2
stressed ['strest]: **be stressed out** *(informal)* im Stress sein 5.4
stretch [stretʃ] Strecke E1.3
strict [strɪkt] streng 5.SS.3
strong [strɒŋ] stark GS.5a
stuck [stʌk]: **be stuck in** stecken (bleiben), festsitzen 10.1b; **get stuck in** festsitzen 5.4
stupid ['stjuːpɪd] blöde, dumm 10.2a
subscription [səb'skrɪpʃən] Abonnement 5.5
such [sʌtʃ] so, solch, derart 8.SS.2
suffer from ['sʌfə frəm] leiden an/unter 5.3
sufferer ['sʌfərə] Leidende/r, Leidtragende/r 5.3
summer sale ['sʌmə ˌseɪl] Sommerschlussverkauf 9.3a
summit ['sʌmɪt] Gipfel E1.3
sunset ['sʌnset] Sonnenuntergang 7.2a
suntan ['sʌntæn] Sonnenbräune 4.TV; **get a suntan** braun werden 4.TV
supplement ['sʌplɪmənt] *hier:* Zuschlag 3.TV
supply [sə'plaɪ] Vorrat 5.5
surprising [sə'praɪzɪŋ] überraschend 4.LC
sweat [swet] Schweiß; schwitzen 10.TV
syllable ['sɪləbəl] Silbe 1.SS.2

T

tag [tæg]: **play tag** Fangen spielen 11.TV; **question tag** Frageanhängsel 5.2a
tails *(pl.)* [teɪlz] *hier:* Zahl 12.2b
take (took, taken) [teɪk (tʊk, 'teɪkən)] *hier:* ergreifen 5.1; *hier:* beanspruchen, benötigen, dauern 5.4; **take a risk** ein Risiko eingehen 9.1; **do/get/take exercise** sich bewegen, Sport treiben 5.TV; **take part** teilnehmen 10.3; **take the dog for a walk** Gassi gehen 1.TV; **take up** benötigen; anfangen; aufnehmen 6.1
task [tɑːsk]: **household task** Aufgabe/Arbeit im Haushalt 6.2
tattoo [tə'tuː] Tätowierung 2.4
technician [tek'nɪʃən] Techniker/in, Facharbeiter/in 8.SS.4
teethe [tiːð] zahnen 1.4a
telephone answering machine ['telɪfəʊn‿ˌɑːnsərɪŋ məˌʃiːn] Anrufbeantworter 8.TV
terminate ['tɜːmɪneɪt] beenden, aufhören 3.4
terrified ['terəfaɪd] erschrocken, verängstigt 4.2a
test [test]: **driving test** Fahrprüfung 1.4a
text [tekst] eine SMS schreiben/senden 8.LC
text-flirting ['tekstflɜːtɪŋ] Flirten per SMS 8.LC
That's OK with me. [ˌðæts‿əʊ'keɪ wɪð ˌmiː] Das ist in Ordnung für mich. 2.2a
things like that [ˌθɪŋz laɪk 'ðæt] so was 2.2a
think back [θɪŋk 'bæk] zurückdenken 6.3
thistle ['θɪsəl] Distel E1.1
thunderstorm ['θʌndəˌstɔːm] Gewitter(sturm), Unwetter 7.TV
ticket ['tɪkɪt]: **lottery ticket** Lotterielos 9.4b; **parking ticket** Strafzettel 3.2b; **ticket collector** Fahrkartenschaffner/in, Zugbegleiter/in 3.4
tide [taɪd] Flut, Gezeiten E2.4
tidy up [ˌtaɪdɪ‿'ʌp] aufräumen 1.SS.3
tight-fitting [ˌtaɪt'fɪtɪŋ] genau passend 11.TV
time [taɪm]: **by this time** *hier:* mittlerweile, inzwischen 3.4; **leisure time** Freizeit 6.LC; **on time** pünktlich 1.1; **time off** Freizeit 2.2a; **under time pressure** unter Zeitdruck 5.4; **time-consuming** zeitraubend 6.TV
tissue ['tɪʃuː] Papiertuch, Taschentuch 10.1a
tone [təʊn] Klang, Ton(fall) 2.SST
tongue [tʌŋ]: **mother tongue** Muttersprache E2.3; **get one's tongue around** etwas nicht aussprechen können, sich die Zunge fast abbrechen E1.2
tool [tuːl]: **gardening tool** Gartengerät 9.3a
top [tɒp]: **come top** an erste Stelle kommen 4.LC
touch [tʌtʃ]: **lose touch with** Kontakt verlieren mit 2.TV
tour ['tʊə]: **package tour** Pauschalreise, Pauschalurlaub 4.TV
trace [treɪs] verfolgen 4.LC
trade fair ['treɪd ˌfeə] (Fach)Messe, Handelsmesse 1.4a
trail [treɪl]: **ski trail** Skipiste, Loipe 7.2a
trainer ['treɪnə] Ausbilder, Trainer 12.2b
training ['treɪnɪŋ]: **in-service training** Ausbildung am Arbeitsplatz, berufsbegleitende Ausbildung 12.TV
transfer ['trænsfɜː]: **bank transfer** Überweisung 9.TV
trolley ['trɒlɪ]: **shopping trolley** Einkaufswagen 9.1
trust [trʌst] (ver)trauen 2.2a
tuition fee [tjʊ'ɪʃən ˌfiː] Studiengebühr
tumble dryer [ˌtʌmbəl 'draɪə] Wäschetrockner 8.TV
tuned ['tjuːnd]: **stay tuned** dran bleiben 2.2a
turn [tɜːn]: **miss a turn** eine Runde aussetzen 12.2b
turn [tɜːn]: **turn over** umdrehen 12.2a; **turn up** auftauchen, erscheinen 4.4
two-thirds [ˌtuː'θɜːdz] zwei Drittel 4.LC
type in [taɪp‿'ɪn] eintasten, eintippen 5.4

U

ugly ['ʌglɪ] hässlich 7.TV
unbelievable [ˌʌnbɪ'liːvəbəl] unglaublich, nicht zu fassen 3.4
understanding [ˌʌndə'stændɪŋ] verständnisvoll 10.SS.2
understood [ʌndə'stʊd]: **make oneself understood** sich verständlich machen 2.3a
undeveloped [ˌʌndɪ'veləpt] nicht entwickelt E2.2a
uneasy [ʌn'iːzɪ] unbehaglich, unruhig 10.1b
unforgettable [ˌʌnfə'getəbəl] unvergesslich 12.2b
unique [juː'niːk] einzig(artig), einmalig E1.3
unreliable [ˌʌnrɪ'laɪəbəl] unzuverlässig 3.TV
unspoilt [ˌʌn'spɔɪlt] unberührt 4.TV
unwind (unwound, unwound) [ʌn'waɪnd (ʌn'waʊnd, ʌn'waʊnd)] (sich) entspannen 6.5
urgent ['ɜːdʒənt]: **urgent call** dringendes Gespräch 8.TV
used [juːst]: **get used to** sich gewöhnen an 4.4

V

vacation *(AE)* [və'keɪʃən]: **on vacation** im Urlaub E1.2
vacuum cleaner ['vækjʊəm ˌkliːnə] Staubsauger 8.TV
valley ['vælɪ] Tal E1.3
value ['væljuː]: **get good value for money** etw. für sein Geld bekommen 9.SS.3
varied ['veərɪd] abwechslungsreich, verschieden(artig) E2.4
variety [və'raɪətɪ] Vielfalt, Auswahl 5.5

vehicle ['vi:ɪkəl] Fahrzeug 3.TV
vibrate [vaɪ'breɪt] vibrieren 2.SS.2
viewing habit [ˌvju:ɪŋ 'hæbɪt] Fernsehgewohnheit 1.1
visit ['vɪsɪt]: **be well worth a visit** sehr wohl einen Besuch wert sein E1.3
visually ['vɪʒʊəlɪ] visuell; seh- 10.LC
vocal chords *(pl.)* ['vəʊkəl kɔ:dz] Stimmbänder 2.SS.2
vocational [vəʊ'keɪʃənəl] beruflich, Berufs- 12.LC
voiced [vɔɪst] stimmhaft 2.SS.2
voiceless ['vɔɪsləs] stimmlos 2.SS.2
volume ['vɒlju:m] Band, Nummer 5.3
vote for ['vəʊt ˌfɔ:] (ab)stimmen für E1.K
voucher ['vaʊtʃə] Gutschein 5.5

W

walk [wɔ:k]: **take the dog for a walk** Gassi gehen 1.TV
war [wɔ:] Krieg 11.1a
washbasin ['wɒʃˌbeɪsən] Waschbecken 8.4
wasp [wɒsp] Wespe 10.1b
waste [weɪst] verschwenden 9.TV
water ['wɔ:tə]: **holy water** Weihwasser 4.4
way [weɪ] *hier:* Methode GS.5a
weak [wi:k] schwach 10.SS.3
weight [weɪt]: **lose weight** abnehmen 5.2a; **put on weight** zunehmen, Gewicht ansetzen 5.TV
welcome ['welkəm]: **make s.o. welcome** jdn. sehr freundlich aufnehmen 4.4
well [wel]: **be well worth a visit** sehr wohl einen Besuch wert sein E1.3
wet [wet] nass, feucht, regnerisch E2.4
whale [weɪl] Wal E2.4
whenever [wen'evə] wann auch immer; so oft 9.2
whereas [weər'æz] während, wohingegen 1.1
wherever [weər'evə] wo(hin) auch immer E2.4
while [waɪl]: **for a while** eine Zeit lang 1.6
Will do. ['wɪl ˌdu:] Mach ich. 1.4b
wipe off [waɪp‿'ɒf] wegwischen 10.1a
within [wɪð'ɪn] drin, im Innern, innerhalb E1.3
wonder ['wʌndə] sich fragen 2.SS.3
wood [wʊd] *hier:* Wald 7.TV
worth [wɜ:θ]: **be well worth a visit** sehr wohl einen Besuch wert sein E1.3
worthwhile [ˌwɜ:θ'waɪl] erstrebenswert, lohnend 6.TV
wreath [ri:θ]: **Advent wreath** Adventskranz 12.1
wrinkle ['rɪŋkəl] Falte, Runzel 11.5

Y

youth hostel ['ju:θ ˌhɒstl] Jugendherberge 4.1

Acknowledgements

The material reproduced in this book has been taken from the following sources:

Illustrations

Jürgen Bartz, München: page 35, 62 – Fran Jordan, Ilkley: page 13, 26, 44, 53

Photographs

Arco Digital Images, Lünen: page 63 (left) – artur/Florian Monheim: cover – Avenue Images GmbH, Hamburg: page 54 (bottom), 60 (top), 62 (left) – Bluewater, Kent: page 74 – www.britainonview.com: page 35 (left), 37 (top middle) (left) – Cartoon Stock Ltd., Bath: page 43 (bottom) – Corbis GmbH, Düsseldorf: page 4 (bottom, Lisa M McGeady) (3rd from bottom, Touhig Sion/Corbis Sygma) (top, Tom Stewart), 5 (2nd from bottom, Richard Cummins), 6 (top, H. Armstrong Roberts), 8 (Tom Stewart), 9 (Tom Stewart), 11 (background, Koopman), 14 (bottom, Corbis Sygma), 19 (left, Touhig Sion/Corbis Sygma) (bottom right, Lee Cohen), 20 (Paul Barton), 23 (left, Michel Setboun), 24 (Michael S. Lewis), 27 (bottom, Lisa M McGeady), 28 (Royalty-Free), 31 (Alen MacWeeney), 38 (top, L. Clarke), 47 (Richard Cummins), 50 (Pierre Perrin/Corbis Sygma), 52 (Eric Robert/Corbis Sygma), 54 (top left, H. Armstrong Roberts) (right, Peter Poby), 56 (Tom Stewart), 62 (right, Staffan Widstrand), 63 (right, Nik Wheeler), 67 (Royalty-Free) – Corel Stock Photo Library: page 4 (2nd from bottom), 6, 15, 22, 23 (right), 27 (middle), 34 (bottom), 36, 37, 39, 40, 46, 48, 62 (top), 64, 65, 70, 71 – Müller/f1online, Frankfurt: page 55 – Sally and Richard Greenhill, London: page 7 – IFA Bilderteam GmbH, München: page 5, 42 (bottom right) – Joker Bildagentur, Köln: page 60 (bottom) – Iwona Kul-Federspiel, München: page 75 – Langenscheidt ELT Archiv, München: page 66, 72 – Ledingham Mark: page 4, 38 (bottom) – Bettina Lindenberg, München: page 12 (left), 30, 42 (bottom middle) – Bildarchiv Mauritius, Mittenwald: page 4 (2nd from top), 5, 6 (2nd from top), 11 (top) (left), 12 (right), 51, 58 – dia/mediacolors: page 33 – Norbert Michalke, Berlin: page 9 (top) – Tourism New Zealand, Wellington: page 69 – PA Photos Ltd., London: page 4 (3rd from top), 6, 16 (right) (middle), 35 (middle) (right), 68, 76 – Picture Press, Hamburg: page 16 (left) – plainpicture Bildagentur, Hamburg: page 11 (right) – Claudia Schwarz, München: page 5 (top), 10 (middle) (right), 11 (bottom), 32 – Iris Steiner, München: page 42 (top) – Superbild Bildarchiv Erich Bach, Grünwald: page 34 (top) – Deutsche Telekom AG, Bonn: page 42 (bottom left), 43 – Andrew Ward, London: page 77 – Peter Widmann: page 27 (top) – Zefa Zentrale Farbbild Agentur GmbH, Düsseldorf: cover (insert), page 3, 14 (top)